EXTRA-HELP LIBRARIANS

A Guide For Success

At Public, Academic And School Libraries

Celma de Faria Luster

Open Vista Press
Petaluma, CA

Aos meus pais,
Antonio e Almerinda
and to
my parents-in-law,
Robert and Helen.

Copyright © 2013 by Celma de Faria Luster

All rights reserved. No portions or the entirety of this book may be reproduced without the written consent of the publisher.

Open Vista Press
P.O. Box 517
Petaluma, CA 94953-0517

This is a work of non-fiction. Although the author and publisher have made every effort to ensure that the information in this book was correct at press time, changes may occur that are beyond their responsibilities. Therefore, the author and publisher do not assume any liability related to the information in this book.

Publisher's Cataloging-in-Publication Data

Luster, Celma de Faria.
  Extra-help librarians : a guide for success at public, academic and school libraries / Celma de Faria Luster.
    p. cm.
  Includes bibliographical references and index.
  ISBN: 978-0-9889242-1-5
  1. Library science—Vocational guidance—United States. 2. Public librarians. 3. School librarians. 4. Academic librarians. I. Title.
Z682.35.V62 L87 2013
023—dc23

2013903020

Cover Page Design: Laurie Ferguson
Layout Design: Gina Bostian

CONTENTS

TABLES viii
INTRODUCTION ix

1 | PROFESSIONAL PROFILE 1

EDUCATION 1
Librarian Competencies 4
CAREER 5
Job Titles 5
Job Categories 6
EXTRA-HELP LIBRARIAN 7
Category Terminology 7
Job Description 8
Profile 8
Position Advantages & Disadvantages 10
JOB SEARCH 17
Basic Considerations 18
Job Postings 19
Job Description Aspects 21
Job Application 22
Interview Planning 25
EMPLOYMENT CONSIDERATIONS 27
Wages 27
Organizational Chart Placement 29
Training & Professional Development 30
Schedule Management 31
Work Ethics 36
Stress 37
Library Open Hours 38
Performance Evaluation 39
Workers Retention 40
Professional Advancement 40
Budget 42
Union Membership 43
Chapter 1 References 43

2 | LIBRARIES OVERVIEW 45

- LIBRARY MISSION, VISION & STRATEGIC PLAN 46
- CLASSIFICATION SYSTEMS 46
- LOCATION & LAYOUT 47
- JOB CONSIDERATIONS 47
  - Responsibilities 47
  - Services & Priorities 48
  - Assigned Projects 49
  - Collection Development 50
  - Communication 56
  - Gaming 61
  - Potential Problems 63
  - Staff Relations 65
  - Institutional Participation 66
  - Professional Associations 66
- REFERENCE & PATRON ASSISTANCE 68
  - Library Catalog 69
  - Technology & Equipment Assistance 71
  - Diversity 75
  - Disabled Persons 76
  - Senior Services 76
  - Volunteers, Friends of the Library & Library Foundation . . . 78
  - Intellectual Freedom & Censorship 79
  - Copyright 80
  - Marketing 80
- *Chapter 2 References* 84

3 | PUBLIC LIBRARIES 87

- ORGANIZATION 88
  - Library Missions 88
  - Public Library Issues 88
  - Organizational Structure 89
- PATRONS 91
- LIBRARIAN RESPONSIBILITIES & LIBRARY SERVICES 94
  - Collection 94
  - Programs & Activities 96
  - Readers Advisory 96
  - Book Discussion 97
  - Non-English & Bilingual Services 97
  - Referrals 99
  - Tax Forms 100
  - Archives 100
  - Homeschooling & Tutoring 101
  - Technology Management 102
- *Chapter 3 References* 103

4 | ACADEMIC LIBRARIES 105

ORGANIZATION 105
- Job Structure 106
- Librarian Benefits 106
- Library Locations 108
- Academic Library Issues 108

PATRONS 110

LIBRARIAN RESPONSIBILITIES 114
- Reference & Instruction 115

Chapter 4 References 126

5 | SCHOOL LIBRARIES 127

ORGANIZATION 128
- Job Titles 128
- Professional Credentials & Qualifications . . . 129
- Practical & Theoretical Issues 130

LIBRARIAN RESPONSIBILITIES 131
- General & Specific Areas 131
- Special Events 133
- Collection Organization 135

PATRONS 138

IMMERSION STRATEGIES 149

Chapter 5 References 150

APPENDIXES 151

BIBLIOGRAPHY 155

WEBLIOGRAPHY 158

INDEX 163

ACKNOWLEDGEMENTS 166

ABOUT THE AUTHOR 167

TABLES

1.1	*Online Classes Evaluation*	page 2
1.2	*Wage Samples*	28
2.1	*Collections & Formats by Library Type*	52
2.2	*Librarian's Associations*	67
2.3	*Listservs by Area of Interest*	68
3.1	*Collection Code Abbreviations*	95

Introduction

Librarians have been romanticized in books and movies with an emphasis on their knowledge, behavior and appearance and mixing reality and fantasy. Sophia Belzer wrote a classic example, *The Substitute Librarian.* As a protagonist it had an Extra-Help Librarian, Ms. Eckhardt. She is one of the few fiction characters of this category. In non-fiction the information about this librarian category is limited too, even though the profession fulfills important roles in libraries, such as temporarily replacing other librarians when they are not able to perform their functions. Therefore, our investigation aims to expand the focus on the Extra-Help Librarian profile and their work in the public, school and academic library settings.

Libraries have personnel systems to manage the replacement of staff on short notices or for longer periods of time. Their size, personnel structure and budget are factors that influence the type of system in place. The terminology used to describe the Extra-Help Librarian's position changes from institution to institution, but the concept is basically the same. In public and school libraries they are often known as substitute librarians and in academic libraries they are adjunct librarians. Considering these variations, for this book's purpose we combined all of them under the category of Extra-Help Librarians. From here on throughout this book that is the term used. The objective here is not to discuss which terminology is the most appropriate, but to provide information about the professional, define their similarities, present theoretical and practical issues as well as other insights they might encounter in the workplace.

This book provides a glimpse at a unique librarian category. Extra-Help Librarians generally provide occasional support to institutions when needs emerge. Many of the situations, such as staff absence, will be commented on to convey the importance of this professional. The content could benefit some groups. Anyone who is thinking about pursuing a library degree would be able to evaluate educational requirements, learn basic librarianship concepts and real aspects of the job. Students already in a Masters in Library and Information Science program, could through the information contained here, capture a broader overview of the profession in addition to specificities that are not usually discussed in Library School. Recent librarian graduates might consider the Extra-Help Librarian position as a first employment opportunity, a venue to gain experience and/or get an edge over job applicants when other positions become available. MLIS professors, library administrators and librarians in general can obtain further insights about staffing issues.

Research and personal experience overlaps throughout the theory and facts contained in this book. Working as an Extra-Help Librarian for several years, and more recently also as a part-time employee in a public library, made the differences between the categories clearer to the author. Other experiences as a library school student, an intern, a volunteer and a parent also contributed to the observations expressed in the following five chapters. Aiming to reduce confusion and repetition, Chapter 1 delineates the Extra-Help Librarian profile and related issues, Chapter 2 gives general information about their work in public, academic and school libraries, Chapter 3 narrows to their practice in public libraries, Chapter 4 focuses on their work at academic libraries and Chapter 5 introduces their dynamics at a school library. Each chapter has its own Chapter Reference section. Samples of Extra-Help Librarian's job postings are included in the Appendix. In all chapters we used the term "patrons" instead of users or clientele, as preferred by some institutions and professionals, for uniformity's sake.

This research is meant to be an overview of librarianship basic concepts and of issues Extra-Help Librarians may face in libraries mentioned. As comprehensive as we meant to be, there are many other aspects to be studied and developed in the future. We hope this is the beginning of many more initiatives which will extend the knowledge and recognition of these professionals.

Overall, considering the demands of the work, it is noteworthy to say that the Extra-Help Librarian position requires from the professional a certain mind set, stamina and focus. It has its demands, but there are many rewards too. Hopefully, the advantages will outweigh the disadvantages for those intrigued by the possibilities that the position offers. It was from a positive experience and outlook that this research materialized.

Best wishes on your own journey.

EXTRA-HELP LIBRARIANS

PROFESSIONAL PROFILE 1

Staffing is an important management issue which involves aspects such as hiring, training, evaluating and employment termination. However, also key is the daily maintenance of the staff needed to keep libraries open and having the necessary number of workers to provide the expected services. In this case, librarians working in various types of libraries and departments often need the assistance of temporary personnel. There are many reasons for this, personal and professional, and assistance can be for a different length of time. In this chapter, we will learn about Extra-Help Librarians who replace the permanent librarian staff whenever necessary and handle other temporary projects. Assuming that they are not well-known, the focus is on their education, the steps followed when choosing to pursue a Library Science degree and earning the degree and then looking for a job in the field. In the process, characteristics are defined and work issues pertinent to the category are presented.

Education

A Master's in Library and Information Science (MLIS/MLS) is required to become a fully certified librarian. Schools accredited by the American Library Association (ALA) provide courses that fulfill basic professional knowledge in the field. The directory of these accredited schools is available through the ALA website, http://www.ala.org/accreditedprograms/directory. There are unaccredited schools, but graduates usually encounter limited employment opportunities. Consequently, it is advisable to evaluate personal goals and professional librarian career advantages and disadvantages before considering school programs. Some of the steps to take into account involve:

- Research the profession
- Check on School Library and Information Science programs
- Request informational interviews with working librarians and library administrators to talk about their practice (duties, satisfaction level, etc.) and professional job prospects
- Analyze the information to find out if it fits your interests and expectations

- Consider instruction type (long distance, mix of online and face-to-face)
- Submit applications to Universities with School of Library Science programs

The type of class environment that library schools offer has become a factor of increasing importance. Long distance classes through online access are replacing face-to-face instruction. Many of the Library Science programs offered nowadays are online-based. A self-evaluation to identify a person's preferred learning styles might be helpful. Also an examination of the pros and cons of online classes (Rockler-Gladen, 2006), see table below, is recommended before committing to a program.

ADVANTAGES	DISADVANTAGES
· Eliminates commuting time · Flexibility & convenience · Self-paced learning · Eliminate scheduling conflicts of work, study, and family · Supplement college classes · Wide variety of classes · Easy application process · Easy contact with faculty through email and live chat · Accommodates various learning styles · Empower students: self-reliance and confidence · Embedded information into class syllabus	· Lack of supervision · Procrastination · Cost – often more expensive · Required computer access and skills · Limitations on class credit transfer to other colleges · Isolation from student community · Unmotivated students fall behind · Students are more likely to get confuse with the course organization (sections, deadlines, applied bibliography) · Impersonal relations · Dependence on technology skills · High learning curve

Table 1.1 Online Classes Evaluation

Once accepted into a program, the next important step is to do advanced degree planning of core and elective classes, based on requirements, preferences, availability and rotations, fitting them into a timeframe. Core classes teach the fundaments of the profession and some curriculum examples (SJSU-SLIS, 2012; Eberts, 2009) include:

- Information and Society
- Information Retrieval
- Online Social Networking: Technology and Tools
- Information Organizations and Management
- Research Methods
- History of books and printing
- Intellectual Freedom and Censorship
- Culminating Experience or Final Project

Electives classes are based on relevant library issues and personal interests on specific subjects of library types—also known as "tracks" (http://sites01.lsu.edu/wp/slis/libraries/; http://les.appstate.edu/programs/library-science/programs-study) specialization is pursued attending classes that focus on certain areas as follows:

- Public Librarianship
  Public Library Issues
  Public Budgeting

- Academic Librarianship
  Information Literacy Instruction
  Research and Resources

- School Librarianship
  Strategic Administration of School Media Resources and Services
  Collaborative Media Program Planning and Evaluation

It might be prudent to learn about each library type, obtaining a more general, broader perspective of the profession, instead of focusing on just one. This curricular approach widens the options when seeking library employment. Work on the core classes and plan the rest of the course. Check the school's recommended track of classes and find out which ones are common to all tracks and take them. For instance, reference, collection development, online searching and cataloging are usually offered to all tracks. Next, take desired elective classes that add skills needed to perform on the job.

Another aspect to consider is that many students already work in a library in other positions and there are also those that have a strong interest in a specific type of library. In such cases, the most common choices are core classes combined with library "track" electives. An academic track includes classes on Academic Library Issues, Instruction Design, and Research Methods. Classes on youth and children's literature and programming are important to those interested in public and school libraries.

In times of economic crisis and a shrinking university budget, class schedules are also affected. Timing is of the essence to choose classes because of pre-requisite, class rotation, and schedule limitations. Not all classes are offered every semester and prioritization between classes needed and wanted is necessary to keep an adequate balance. At least in the first semester, it is best to avoid class overload until acquiring a sense of how much time is needed to be allocated to studying, doing school assignments, and perhaps working.

Students should also be attentive to other learning opportunities beyond the classroom to acquire a broader view of the profession, learn about the marketplace and develop contacts through initiatives like:

- Research on libraries and other institutions that employ librarians or use their skills
- Apply to internships or projects with potential to add perspective into the profession
- Work in a library in positions such as a paraprofessional, student aid, library page or volunteer
- Join professional associations, attend conferences and workshops, and library publications
- Subscribe to online discussion groups, listservs, and blogs

LIBRARIAN COMPETENCIES

Institutions create their mission, vision and goals, and set expectations for their employee for each category. Instruments such as job descriptions include employee competencies that can serve as a guide to future performance evaluation. Librarians' responsibilities in the workplace change depending on the type of library and specificities of the job but their competencies are defined in broader terms. They relate to the level of professional knowledge, abilities and skills applied to the job for which they are hired. Basic competencies include critical thinking, organizational and interpersonal skills, technology experience, and field knowledge (McNeil, 2001). ALA's Core Competences of Librarianship emphasizes these eight aspects: foundations of the profession, information resources, organization of recorded knowledge and information, technological knowledge and skills, reference and user services, research, continuing education and lifelong learning, administration and management (http://www.ala.org/educationcareers/sites/ala.org.educationcareers/files/content/careers/corecomp/corecompetences/finalcorecompstat09.pdf).

A librarian's core competencies in many areas may be used as guidelines for hiring, training and performance. Consequently, they are of great importance and a school's and a student's responsibilities in getting prepared to enter the marketplace can not be overlooked. Technology knowledge, for instance, has become a necessity for librarians because libraries are increasingly facilitating patrons' access to the internet and engaging in technology based services. Therefore, librarians are adapting and adopting new professional standards that require skills to handle new software, hardware, and mobile devices (Thompson, 2009). Based on these competencies, librarians can identify how well they use technology at work.

Career

JOB TITLES

A Master's in Library and Information Science (MLIS) offers a wide range of work opportunities which translate into a variety of titles and tasks. There are traditional librarians' areas such as reference, catalogue, collection development, and outreach. As librarians embrace new technologies additional skills are needed. The profession is diversifying and expanding into instruction, electronic resources management, webmaster, and many branches of information seekers and providers. Position titles listed below are a small sample that illustrates how diverse the applications of library science have become.

- Adjunct Librarian Faculty Pool
- Adult Reference Librarian
- Automated Systems Librarians
- Children's Librarian
- Coordinator of Library Instruction
- Coordinator of Reference Services
- Collection Development Librarian for Youth Materials
- Coordinator of Children's, Young Adult or Youth Services
- Database Coordinators, Developers and Trainers
- Data Librarian for Business and Economics
- Educational Liaisons for Vendors
- Information Architects
- Information Consultants/Information Brokers
- Information Literacy Instructor
- Instructional Librarian
- Information Services Librarian
- Law Librarian
- Librarian Cataloger
- Library Consultant
- Librarian Manager
- Librarian Substitute
- Media Specialist
- Medical Librarian
- Outreach Librarian
- Project Managers
- Public School Library Coordinator
- Public Services Librarians
- Reference Librarian
- Reference Tool Developers
- Regional or State Youth Specialist
- Research Librarian
- School District Library Coordinator
- School Media Specialist
- School Librarian
- Social Work Librarian
- Systems Analysts
- Teacher Librarian
- Technical Services Librarian
- Technology Coordinators and Trainers
- Usability Testers
- Virtual Reference Librarians
- Web 2.0 Developers
- Web Content Managers
- Web Designers
- Webmaster
- Web Project Managers
- Wine Librarian
- Young Adult or Teen Librarian

Evaluation of a particular position based on the job description can be easily accessible through various library job advertisement sites such as ALA's JobLIST, a state's libraries website, and various other library job postings online, as well as professional magazines and journals in print.

JOB CATEGORIES

Library personnel include the director or dean, librarians, and support staff, such as library associate/library assistant/associate specialist, library technical assistant/technical assistant, and clerks in various functions. The most important factor that differentiates librarians from other library personnel is that they earned a masters' degree in Library and Information Science from an institution accredited by the American Library Association (ALA). Librarians have distinct responsibilities and compensation depending on their experience and position. They are employed in specific categories, such as entry-level or supervisor for instance.

Extra-Help Librarian is one of the various librarian categories. Not all libraries utilize them, but they work in a variety of areas and departments, depending on the librarian skills and a library's work demands. When they are at work there is not apparent distinction between them and other librarians on the staff. Extra-Help Librarian category specificities are not as well researched as other librarian staff. Articles have been produced focusing on relevant issues in the academic setting. For instance, these articles discuss an "alternative staffing model" which would release librarians from their duties at times to attend training, referring to who these professionals would be, where they would come from, training needs required and budget implications (Massis, 2008). Also, focusing on re-engaging part-time librarians through training, integration and better communication (Jones, 2011) meant that more detailed professional aspects needed to be developed. As a result of this lack of information, we will expand to a more in-depth study of Extra-Help Librarians and will trace their profile. Other information about their work at public, academic and school libraries is discussed in subsequent chapters.

Extra-Help Librarian

CATEGORY TERMINOLOGY

There are several job title designations of librarians working on a part-time basis, most frequently on temporary assignments. Each institution has its own preferred terminology to describe the professional that replaces a regular employee for a determined period of time in occasions such as vacation. In addition to job title differences, job descriptions and work responsibilities vary as well. A compilation of job titles used include the following samples.

> Librarian Substitute
> Librarian Substitute – Intermittent
> Substitute Library Staff – Librarian Part-Time
> Librarian Part-Time Substitute
> Part-Time Temporary Librarian
> On-Call
> Hourly
> Temporary as Needed
> Extra-Help
> Adjunct Librarian

Whichever terminology is used, they are classified as part-time employees. There are a number of differences depending on the library type, their placement in the organization, and the category in which they are classified. Also, distinctions exist between the regular part-time librarian and those providing occasional support. The first group, regular part-time, usually has consistent, regular scheduled hours. Many institutions provide them partial medical benefits based on the number of hours worked, participation in a retirement plan, and a certain degree of job security. Extra-Help Librarians temporarily replace regular librarians who are out for an appointment for a few hours or a few days in a row, for a few months due to surgery, or even possibly for an extended period when disability is involved. Such circumstances generate part-time or full-time assignments with a potential number of hours for a determined period of time depending on the predictability of the situation. Examples of stable temporary work in long-term assignments include replacing a librarian on sabbatical or pregnancy leave, as well as taking an open position while the search for a permanent employee is in process.

Each assignment is likely to be different and that is the beauty and curse of the Extra-Help Librarians category. Their rights and responsibilities vary from one institution to another. Advantages and disadvantages needs to be analyzed individually, especially in regards to regular assignments such as teaching a course for a semester or committing to last minute notice to short-term temporary work. Guidance on specific information on benefits—or lack thereof—can be obtained by checking with the employer's Human Resources Department, the Union, or the Part-Time Librarians Association (http://part-time-librarians.net).

JOB DESCRIPTION

Generally librarians work a regular full-time schedule or a part-time schedule. Their hours are predetermined and they receive employment benefits such as vacations, sick-time and medical care. Extra-Help Librarians, on the other hand, fulfill the same educational requirements—possession of a Masters in Library and Information Science—and related skills, but in administrative terms they are grouped in a separate category due to their distinct characteristics. Flexible work hours and limited or no benefits are employment aspects that differentiate them from their co-workers.

Extra-Help Librarians positions can offer an enriching experience for flexible professionals who are open to frequent changes. Where and when they work, who they work with, what kind of tasks they do, and how they do them from branch to branch or campus to campus is part of their context. They understand staffing complexities, appreciate community differences, and adapt to the way local leadership apply rules and procedures. The variety of work that Extra-Help Librarians are trained to do and the experience acquired on the job gives them a unique outlook.

The abilities necessary to Extra-Help Librarians to do the job well start with a positive attitude. In addition, it is critical that they are comfortable with people and technology. Since it is common for them not to be regularly at one location they often aim to blend in and provide seamless service to patrons. Therefore, their knowledge of the collection and location within the building, their customer service skills, and technology competence facilitate interactions with patrons.

PROFILE

Librarianship attracts people from many fields and many of them choose it as a second—or even later—career. Such diversity promotes a fluidity of ideas and expertise, and it brings together a mix of professionals in various phases of life. That is even more accentuated in the Extra-Help Librarians category and considering some of their similarities they were divided in three groups: new librarians, retirees, and transitioners. The characteristics of each group are presented in the next few pages.

NEW LIBRARIANS

While in library school students spend most of their time learning librarianship theories and practices. Internships and practicum are the most common opportunities available to obtain some experience in libraries, unless they have worked previously in other library positions. Once they graduate as a librarian, they qualify for entry-level positions (e.g. no experience necessary) and higher if their previous careers fulfill other category requirements. An Extra-Help Librarian's position is another alternative. Such job openings are attractive to new librarians because it provides such a great range of practical learning opportunities. They offer a glimpse into a library or library system through short and long term assignments, and can lead to full-time and part-time positions. The time spent in main libraries, campus or branch, and internal departments give new librarians various responsibilities that they would not be able to be exposed to otherwise. In addition, an Extra-Help Librarian's training provides an in-depth understanding of the library's structure and librarian functions.

RETIREES

Librarians are generally happy with their careers (Miller, 2011). Many of them even stay on the job for years past retirement age. Once they decide they want to retire, some of them look for ways to continue in the field without all the responsibilities of a full-time position. Post-retirement possibilities involve activities for limited hours or part-time employment. Besides volunteering, librarians often enter into Extra-Help Librarian pools fulfilling their desire to stay active in the profession. The position also provides the advantage of earning extra income. Retired professionals are desirable as Extra-Help Librarians because of their expertise in the field. Libraries need to invest less time training them, focusing more on library procedures and technology currency, in case they retired from a different library. It is not uncommon for retirees to enter the Extra-Help Librarian pool of the library they worked for as a full-time employee before retirement.

Interested librarians nearing retirement and looking for future options should take into account their personal interests and financial caps (e.g. IRS rules, pension allowances, etc.), especially when it involves earning extra income. Usually, such concerns are investigated during the retirement process through taxation and pension planning. Retirees' reemployment follows the Internal Revenue Service guidelines (http://www.irs.gov/publications/p721/ar02.html#en_US_2011_publink1000228236) aligned with procedures of each specific organization. The University of Akron guidelines for retiree reemployment is an example (http://www.uakron.edu/hr/benefits/reemployment-procedures-for-retirees.dot). Other implications are presented in the University of Washington policy (http://staffweb.lib.washington.edu/units/human-resources/current/retired-re-employeed/

retire-reemploy-libn). Also, regulations of the Maryland State Retirement Agency and the Anne Arundel County—http://www.aacounty.org/Personnel/Pension/FAQReemployment.cfm—offer useful information to better comprehend retirees' income boundaries and job limitations when seeking Extra-Help Librarians positions. Librarians who are Union affiliates are able to get additional support in navigating this process.

TRANSITIONERS

A variety of reasons draw librarian professionals to became Extra-Help Librarians for short or long term. There are times when librarians need to focus on personal issues that might require them to withdraw from their professional career temporarily. Some choose to move to another area, raise children, or care for their elders. Extra-Help Librarian positions are ideal for librarians making these choices because of the advantages that it offers in time management, especially in regards to flexibility. Librarians searching for a full-time position or returning to librarianship can also find ways to earn an income and bring their skills up-to-date. An Extra-Help Librarian position might be a perfect option when personal responsibilities are overwhelming and time is needed. A chance to stay professionally current, have time for personal demands, and earn supplemental income is possible in this position.

There are many cases of librarians who at one point in their careers were Extra-Help Librarians and were hired into other librarian positions. An example is the librarian Marrian Matthews in Los Angeles—http://articles.latimes.com/2003/jul/06/local/me-matthews6 (Oliver, 2003)—but there are other librarians even in your own neighborhood library who have gone through this transition process. It is not unusual either for full-time and part-time librarians to decide to change their employment status into Extra-Help Librarian, a reverse option. It is relevant to mention that part-time librarians and librarian associates are also categories that may participate in the Extra-Help Librarians pool. The library's Human Resources can clarify such inclusions when they occur. In general, they might work occasionally, adding more hours to their schedule to supplement their income. Also, some of them are librarians waiting for a full-time position to come open. This regular part-time staff competes for Extra-Help Librarian jobs, especially at the location in which they work regularly. In this case, it facilitates managers' scheduling efforts, since there will be less frequent need to search for other Extra-Help Librarians.

POSITION ADVANTAGE & DISADVANTAGES

Through research and personal experience positive and negative aspects of the Extra-Help Librarians' position were compiled and evaluated with the intent to provide some understanding of the category. It is definitely a valuable position to libraries. They are versatile professionals who support whichever area there is need of staff coverage. They work with a variety of people, learn tasks quickly, and have a chance to show the abilities and qualifications that might be useful in future employment opportunities. Extra-Help Librarians also have difficulties and they seem to be less interconnected with their peers. More aspects related to their position are presented below for further discussion.

ADVANTAGES

Flexibility

One of the most relevant aspects of working as an Extra-Help Librarian is to be able to set your own schedule. However, make the availability attractive to the employer. The process is simple, the more days, nights and weekends available, the higher the chances to be scheduled to work. Personal goals in terms of earning and learning are linked to availability. As far as earnings, just a few hours of work a week might be satisfactory to a retiree, but perhaps not to a new librarian who needs the income or wants more exposure on the job. Such flexibility is a key motivator for workers, allowing individuals to stay professionally active while involved in other interests, reserving free-time to fulfill personal needs or spend it on leisure activities. However, there are libraries that set limitations on how many pay periods the employee decides not to work and the total hours that he/she can work. In case of an extra long withdrawal from work, one might have to reapply for the pool position, which could be closed without notice. Clarify matters with the library's Human Resources Department, or equivalent, since it is best not to overlook details of such nature. Time off could turn out to be a costly free-time, turning such benefit into a problem. In general, flexibility is fundamental to be able to work in this position.

Independence

Extra-Help Librarians work with permanent librarians most of the time. However, there are times when they work with no direct supervision in a project or at the reference desk, or as a solo librarian, having a chance to exercise self-management skills, deciding what to do and when and how. Working solo is challenging and rewarding. It can be difficult at first, but once the rules and procedures are well known it becomes very satisfying. Projects with specific directions and deadlines offer more possibilities to exercise independence. Getting the work done properly demonstrates professional qualifications and provides invaluable chances to earn administrators' trust. It might generate subsequent opportunities for more work and advantages when competing for other job positions. In general, floating from location to location, project to project, working days or nights, gives a sense of freedom from a rigid work schedule. Extra-Help Librarians might work hours that are not desired by permanent staff or supplement work shifts at night, evening and weekend hours. Availability during these hours is often required. Working solo or independently on projects are opportunities to prove responsibility, reliability, and efficiency.

Diverse Environment

Frequent changes in work location provide greater chances to experience a variety of space, resources handling, contact with various communities, staff and users, as well as responsibilities. It is a thriving environment for people that are motivated by new challenges and an unusual schedule. Adaptability to different aspects of the job and to frequent schedule switches is necessary. After working as an Extra-Help Librarian for a while, patterns set in and the comfort level increases because much is learned about expectations, routines, projects and staff at certain branches, departments or campuses. Familiarity with location differences facilitate Extra-Help Librarians to approach the workday in a more predictable and enjoyable manner. Appreciation for the uniqueness of each workplace is a major step to embrace diversity.

Broader Viewpoint

Extra-Help Librarians work frequency, location variety, types of tasks and responsibilities, patrons and staff produce distinct perspectives. Those working in single libraries have the opportunity to really learn the complexities and needs of that location. There is a chance for repeat contact with patrons, development of stronger camaraderie with staff and volunteers, in-depth knowledge of the collection, and more chances to show consistent efficiency at work. Experience acquired working at various places, branches or campus libraries, is more diverse, but collection knowledge and relationships can be more superficial. However, it clearly offers a broad overview, especially of a library system. A combination of these experiences is often possible within the same organization due to short and long term assignments, offering valuable insights. The professional's ability to delineate objective comparisons and apply cross-over strategies benefits the institution. Therefore, such perspectives are advantageous to employers, and to Extra-Help Librarians too, making them more marketable for other positions in any type of library and other institutions that can utilize their skills.

Cross Over Experience

Library needs may provide Extra-Help Librarians opportunities to work in different departments occasionally or on a regular basis. Consequently, in a public library it is not unusual to work in place of a children's librarian and at the adult reference. Depending on the days' schedule, there can be a switch back and forth in matter of hours. In an academic library, work at the reference desk and other areas or projects is also common. Such exposure is interesting and enriching, in particular for new graduates in the Extra-Help pool. In this case, they can learn a lot in a short time, help them decide which area they would like to specialize in, and it can increase their chances of employment. Retirees can be motivated by such an environment as well, enjoying areas that were not part of their responsibilities in past jobs.

Professional Currency

All Extra-Help Librarians (whether retirees, new librarians or workers in transition) need to have an interest in staying up-to-date on the inner workings of the library regarding what is happening, changing or updating. The continuing effort to meet user needs involve innovation and the continuing reshaping of librarians' work. Extra-Help Librarians learn the new approaches on how to serve the community, sharpen their skills on the latest procedures and policies, programs and problems and solutions. The Extra-Help Librarian position requires them to be current on the changes taking place either locally or at other branches and campuses in the system. That can be overwhelming to a degree, but it energizes those that thrive on providing the best service.

Mentor Support

As part of the training process, sometimes a permanent librarian in staff is assigned to mentor Extra-Help Librarians. If that is not the case, perhaps advocating for it might lead to connection with a mentor. This relationship does not have to terminate at a specific date but can develop for as long as both parties recognize the need for it and are willing to continue the relationship. It can be an excellent way to learn how to handle daily routines and task shortcuts, to learn about the organization culture or to even develop a long lasting friendship.

Work Appreciation

When a worker leaves, the institution is often short-handed. Extra-Help Librarians reinstate some normalcy when replacing the worker for a determinate period of time. They are crucial to keep a branch open or a department's work uninterrupted during staff shortage. Appreciation is often expressed by staff, co-workers and managers, especially when the work is done graciously and competently. Extra-Help Librarians' understanding of their responsibilities, positive attitude, initiative and work well-done are the basis for recognition.

Staff Competitiveness

Extra-Help Librarians are often less threatening to local established rules—verbalized or not—and staff informal alliances. Since they usually go to more than one place, mostly for short periods of time, and make sporadic appearances, there is less of a chance to develop ties and be part of or against specific groups. Attentiveness to work space territoriality, power struggles, and suggestions for changes can help maintain cordiality in the workplace. It is best to be less involved in localized matters until the culture is learned and understood. A helpful and non-threatening approach leads to the development of more harmonious work relationships.

Schedule Rotation

Managers attempt to structure staff's schedules in a way that will maximize necessary work and provide the services expected. It is especially challenging to have enough coverage when the library is open long hours, evenings, holidays or weekends. In such cases, staff schedule rotation is needed, and it can be a challenge to cover undesirable days and times, as well as unpredictable situations. Many circumstances impact schedule rotation. Extra-Help Librarians do not take part in it, although they often benefit from it. They are not necessarily governed by such a system directly, because they can block their availability for a certain time or day. On the other hand, schedule rotation actually provides them with opportunities to work. For example, regular librarians might have a personal commitment that falls on a day that they are scheduled to work. Since schedule rotations are not predictable too far in advance, they can lead managers to request Extra-Help Librarians to fill in during that time.

Job Postings Access

Participating in a Extra-Help Librarian pool is an efficient job search strategy. It is a way to learn about a library system and identify the pros and cons of working at the organization. It clarifies personal preferences. For instance, one can evaluate the location desirability, community composition (diverse or more homogenous), co-workers personalities, work ethics, creativity, and other factors. It helps identify how desirable it would be to work daily in a determined location, since it can be difficult to obtain insights of much depth about a job opening when outside of an organization. Therefore, it offers a unique opportunity to evaluate the desirability of upcoming jobs while within the library system.

There are two different types of job postings that can be taken advantage of while already in a Extra-Help Librarian pool. First, library jobs are posted to staff only or initially to staff. If jobs are not filled from within they are advertised to the public. Access to jobs publicized internally increases the chances of staff interested in a permanent position to get hired for full-time or part-time. Extra-Help Librarians have a chance to apply for such opportunities, only competing with other staff categories. Therefore, library associates who are qualified to move up or librarians that want to move laterally usually apply too. Second, another type of job posting comes in the form of long term assignments. These are communicated directly to Extra-Help Librarians. When librarian staff request time off for an extended period of time, Extra-Help Librarians fill the position. A letter, email, or telephone call is generally necessary to formalize the interest in the position.

In sum, it is advantageous to be a library staff member in the Extra-Help Librarian category. The opportunity to be able to apply for internal positions is a great benefit, especially to those who have already decided that the library they work for is the one that they want to continue with. In times when the library budgets are shrinking and fewer positions are available, Extra-Help Librarian positions are even more attractive due to the advantages they offer.

DISADVANTAGES

Hourly Position

Work based on payment of wages per hour has its' drawbacks. In comparison with other workers' wages, the amount paid might seem fine. But looking at paycheck deductions and considering the lack of or the reduction of benefits, Extra-Help Librarian earnings might not seem as attractive. On the other hand, urban libraries or system libraries might have higher demand for the position and offer better payment per hour. Healthy budgets and an adequate number of Extra-Help Librarians can also influence the frequency of work and opportunities to earn a better income. Clearly, the income generated by this employment is meant to be supplementary instead of the only income.

No Overtime

Libraries discourage or do not allow overtime for Extra-Help Librarians. Human Resources may keep a more rigorous record of the category's hours worked weekly or per pay period, as well as the annual employment maximum. This restricts their earnings even more. Supervisors tend to organize staff schedules to avoid incurring overtime. Even when regular staff works extra hours they receive compensation time, making it possible to take personal leave at some other desired point. But do not expect the same privilege, except in staffing emergency cases when other arrangements may be offered. In fact, breaks and meal times are monitored to first fulfill the law about workers rest time, but also to avoid overtime.

No Medical & Dental Benefits

These benefits are provided on a pro-rated basis or not provided at all to library workers. This issue constitutes a major disadvantage of Extra-Help Librarians. Each group—new librarians, transitioners or retirees—is affected at different degrees. Single income employees and those with dependents may feel the impact more closely, because if they do not have even partial benefits it means that payment of private insurance may become necessary. Retirees with coverage through an employer and those who have insurance coverage under a partner's work policy have better arrangements. Overall, it is advisable to consider reduced, or even a lack of medical and dental coverage, on personal finances when applying for the position.

No Vacation, Sick Leave, Sabbatical

Extra-Help Librarians substitute for workers that are on sabbatical, vacation or sick leave and frequently do not have these same paid work benefits themselves. Consider if this is something that makes much difference in terms of personal needs. Not being able to accrue such leave rights can be very difficult for new librarians and transitioners. When there may be a need for these benefits, for medical reasons in particular, reality might force Extra-Help Librarians to work when they would be advised to stay home and nurse themselves back to health.

No Retirement Funds or Pension Plan

Retirement or pension funds are long term benefits that libraries do not usually offer to Extra-Help Librarians. Human Resources can give you further information in advance or during the hiring phase. Even when some percentage of Extra-Help Librarians earnings are withheld for retirement purposes, the total amount earned is small and the percentage is not significant enough for long term plans. Awareness of any contributions to retirement savings is advisable to make informed decisions about the investment or the fund's administrator.

No Job Security & Certainty

Extra-Help Librarians have neither job security nor job certainty. Unless they are protected by union agreements with the library, it means that they are employees at will. Simply, they can be discharged without any specific reason and without compensation. It is common that job certainty does not exist. At certain times jobs come up frequently. It depends on the season, on meetings and conferences and on staff time off. On other occasions, jobs are scarce and they may be delivered with only a few hours' notice. Even long term assignments can be canceled unexpectedly. There are many variables and personal ability to manage a lack of job security and uncertainty is a necessary strength to work in this job category.

No Institutional Involvement

Library workers are generally involved at the institution and professional association level. There are opportunities to participate internally in committees in various areas, such as ethics and collections directives. A chance to attend professional associations' conferences is another common channel of participation. Generally, Extra-Help Librarians do not participate in such professional opportunities because there is no institutional support. Due to the temporary nature of Extra-Help Librarian's work arrangements, libraries tend to make professional participation not available to the category, taking away the responsibility and the reward that emanates from being involved. It could be possible that retirees might not have interest in such involvements. But new librarians may want to participate in committees and attend conferences.

No Decision Making Input

Extra-Help Librarians responsibilities are mostly short-term, temporary and fragmented. This lack of continuity is a barrier to participation in decision making processes and institutional involvement. Few are the opportunities to give input to programs planning, policies and procedures, staff meetings or other options. Regular full-time staff is responsible for setting work priorities and making implementations. An exception occurs when working as a solo librarian. Then, Extra-Help Librarians can manage library staff and have increased responsibilities. They can make more decisions if only temporarily. Such opportunity contributes to professional confidence and may reflect in future career advancement.

Looking from another angle, the impact of lack of opportunities to make decisions requires adjustments from professionals. Retirees, for instance, can be affected personally because they have may worked in positions that were even higher than of those now supervising them. Also, some times they work for a younger staff and it can be hard to adjust to this. However, it can be perceived as liberating not to be the decision maker and carry many of the responsibilities.

JOB SEARCH

Job searching is a process that involves organization, persistence and networking. Developing a plan helps the applicant to keep focused. For instance, the use of technology has improved the access to job postings since they appear in a variety of channels. While listservs, professional and governmental organizations' websites are common sources for job placement, there are still those libraries that use their websites as the main advertising method. Timing is not always the main factor, in particular in libraries that accept applications on a continual basis or at a few times a year. When seeking a job in a specific library, its website and Human Resources Department may provide more detailed information.

The job search process for Extra-Help Librarians does not differ much in regards to the steps used for other librarian positions. A combination of strategies typically produces the needed result. Thus, effective job search approaches generally include the use of some of the following sources:

- Schoolmates, family and friends
- Libraries nationwide
- Professional associations contacts through conferences, meetings, training sessions and social events
- Professional magazines job advertisements
- Library school job placement centers
- Professional listservs job postings
- Job listings on the internet
- Job placement services
- Employment agencies
- ALA guide to libraries' directories and links to websites worldwide

In addition, some institutions and job search websites offer free job opening updates via e-mail through subscription to their service. This remarkable feature facilitates the job search process. As far as Extra-Help Librarian jobs, they are not advertised as often as other library positions and it may be that fellow librarians are the most reliable sources of information when openings become available. However, do the search following the same job search steps, use word-of-mouth, make inquiry calls to Human Resources departments, search the sources mentioned, and remember to use the various terminologies common to the position.

BASIC CONSIDERATIONS

A close scrutiny of the job posting is necessary, as well as a self-evaluation of professional skills and interests to identify matching characteristics. Applicants have to consider relevant aspects of the position, list them and check how they affect personal goals when weighing the viability of the position. Here are some points to think about in the pre-application phase:

- Location (urban, rural, state, country)
- Library type (city, county, law, public, academic)
- Library size (small or large)
- Position level (entry-level, Librarian II, supervisor)
- Responsibilities and expectations
- Salary (minimum accepted, compensation range)
- Benefits needed vs. offered (medical, dental, tuition reimbursement)
- Full-time, part-time, temporary

A librarian's work encompasses a vast array of skills that are linked to position functions and are determined by libraries type. Extra-Help Librarians need the same work skills of regular librarians and may need to apply them to many library areas, some of which include:

Administration
Collection development
Instruction design and presentation
Outreach/Advocacy
Programming
Rare manuscripts and archives
Reference
Research
Specialized collections
Technical services
User services for adults, teens and/or children
Web site design
Instructional content creation

JOB POSTINGS

Human Resources Department in public and school libraries, and Faculty Affairs in academic libraries, are responsible for releasing job opening announcements which is disseminated through channels mentioned in the job search section above. Applications can be geared to single or "pool" positions. This means that there is a vacant position or applications are accepted to be available to work sporadically when there is a need for them. Anyone qualified has a chance to apply to the job opening, following the process described on the posting. Institutions often post internally first, then to the public if the position is not filled by staff or if it requires applicants with a higher level of experience. Even though the latter process involves more time and resources, institutions may expect to attract a greater number of applicants and also a more diverse group if they go outside.

Components & Usage

Job postings are structured to provide the most important information about the position open. It should have many components that intend to provide necessary details about a job to interested librarians. There is not a perfect format, but a variety of them can be used depending on the amount of information provided. An example of each library type in the Appendix illustrates some relevant components. The amount of details differ, however most types of job postings incorporate most or at least some of the following:

> Position title
> Date posted
> Position or job number
> Eligible applicants (internal/external)
> Institution (location, collection, patrons)
> Position location and department
> Category/rank (Librarian I, II, Adjunct)
> Responsibilities/duties
> Professional requirements
> Desired qualifications
> Availability needed
> Compensation/ wages/pay grade
> Closing date
> Interview date
> Starting date
> Documentation required
> Contact person or department
> Application deadline/closing date

Submission preferences and details
Link to the library website

Job postings for Extra-Help Librarians often do not mention benefits such as health, dental, sick time. Assume that if it is not stated, it is not provided, but even then make sure to ask about it. It is common practice to approach such matters later in the interviewing or hiring phase. However, applicants who consider benefits to be crucial could request additional information contacting the Human Resources Department or equivalent office.

Requirements & Qualifications

Professional Requirements

Librarian's job postings content depends upon the type, location and size of the library. Variations depend on the complexity of the functions. However, there are common professional requirements as stated below:

Masters' degree from a school accredited by ALA
Second masters' degree for field specialists
Professional credentials, if applicable
Combination of equivalent experience, education and/or training

In addition to these basic requirements, often Extra-Help Librarian job postings clearly state the need for a professional willing to work nights and weekends. Even though this is a scheduling issue it is nonetheless a requirement stipulated by the institution that needs to be fulfilled.

Desired Qualifications

Public services librarians, regardless of the institution type, usually have personal characteristics and abilities that are very desirable. Job postings usually have a section listing some of the qualities and work experience related to the job needs. Below is a summary of some desired skills, including personal characteristics and other professional abilities.

- Reliable
- Initiative
- Self-starter
- Team player
- Positive attitude
- Friendly
- Receptive
- Motivation
- Courteous manner
- Organized
- Adaptable
- Problem solver
- Confident
- Cooperative
- Energetic
- Dedicated
- Enthusiastic
- Outgoing
- Handle confidentiality properly
- Accountable

- Work independently
- Patient
- Researcher
- Creative
- Service oriented
- Team player
- Interpersonal skills
- Analytical thinker
- Leadership skills
- Subject expertise
- Effective oral & written communication
- Follow instructions
- Reader
- Learner
- Inquisitive
- Problem solver
- Multi-tasking abilities
- Desire to help others
- Teaching experience
- Technology knowledge
- Years of experience
- Managerial skills

Extra-Help Librarian's experience and commitment to provide excellent service are desired elements. Their attitude toward patrons and co-workers shows their professionalism. In addition, they work in many places, interact with diverse populations, are well informed and know how to handle routine responsibilities and unexpected work. These candidates' skills illustrate desired aspects that employers seek in this category. Also, there are more skills—such as foreign language knowledge, supervision experience and familiarity with specific software—that give the job applicant clues on what could give them an edge over other candidates and also on the possibility for advancement within the organization.

JOB DESCRIPTION ASPECTS

In this section the responsibilities and duties are described in general terms and are not task oriented, but driven by function and responsibilities. Often there is a statement of "typical duties may include, but are not limited to..". This excerpt is especially true for Extra-Help Librarians positions since it is often difficult to list all the responsibilities entailed. It is a position that morphs frequently and the professional needs to be open to the new and unexpected changes that may occur and require them to adjust quickly. Since Extra-Help Librarians work on a variety of locations (main/central, branches, campuses and schools) and to perform different roles and duties (adult and children's reference desk, archives, etc.) do not expect a lot from job descriptions.

Most job descriptions focus on professional qualifications instead of specific tasks. In general, the librarians' and Extra-Help Librarians' job descriptions are very similar, focusing on their educational background, skills and responsibilities. What really differs them are the employment arrangements about work hours, wages and benefit status. Extra-Help Librarian job descriptions based on core competency standards in various knowledge areas is beneficial to employer and employee. The lack of specific job descriptions for the category makes it more difficult to learn about their contributions to the organization, measurement of their productivity and performance evaluation. Job description is an essential tool at two levels. First, it facilitates organizations' efforts to recruit and evaluate the category. Second, it guides Extra-Help Librarians to be better informed about the organization guidelines and expectations, as well as their understanding of their professional rights.

JOB APPLICATION

Once research on the job position is comprehensive and materials are gathered, it is time to put the application package together. Look at everything to get a complete idea of the steps already taken. Review the items to be sure about what is needed to be said and done and is all organized. Make sure all the parts are compiled, filled, reviewed and then submit the application. Here is a basic review guide.

JOB POSTING APPROACH

Review of job posting requires attention to all parts and details. It is important to set a clear approach to this process, including these steps:

- Read and re-read
- Underline important elements, such as matching skills
- Number the documents required to send with the application
- Mark the closing date

Job posting instructions will be explicit about the documents that should be submitted in the application package. Be certain to submit only what is requested at this point. Supplementary documentation might be needed as the selection process moves into various phases.

Submission options

Currently there are choices on how to apply or how to send the application to the institution's Human Resources or Academic Affairs Department. It can be sent by mail, email, or completed online at the applicant's own pace. If a response to a supplementary questionnaire is necessary, be sure to complete it or your application will not be considered. Sometimes hard copy submission requires two sets. E-mail and online application are becoming the most frequent methods of application submission due to their convenience, ease of use and follow up.

Documentation

The following documents are not necessarily all that are required in the job application package. Depending on the type of submission, combinations of a few of them may become part of the submission package. Electronic submission systems tend to simplify the process, offering options to upload or paste a resume. E-mail submission accepts the majority of the documents. The mail submission is the one that requires the most documentation. In all cases, just follow the job posting instructions closely to send the necessary items.

Cover letter

Write the cover letter, also known as letter of interest, giving special attention to the job description's requirements and desired qualifications. Considering the information gathered, personalize the cover letter as much as possible, linking skills and abilities to the job. Acknowledge the other requirements not fulfilled and highlight experiences and learning abilities that could be advantageous to the library. Remember that grammar, format and content are basics of professional looking cover letters.

Resume / Curriculum Vitae

Using one resume for all job applications is easy, but it is considered a poor strategy. As much as possible make your resume fit each position, taking out irrelevant information to the position, adding new information such as courses, webinars or whatever else that show current interests related to the job. Attach the resume when submitting an application via email or online whenever possible. The format might be scrambled when pasting it into forms.

References

Some institutions still require reference letters, while others only request a list of references which may be easier to provide. It can be a delicate situation to ask for reference letters. It is sensible to require them in the interview phase, as a support tool for selection, but it is common for academic libraries to require them as part of the application package.

Diversity Statement

Academic libraries usually require the attachment of a diversity statement along with the other application documents. It should demonstrate the applicant's sensitivity to their diverse community, students, staff, and faculty in terms of race, religion, socio-economic or cultural status, disabilities and sexual orientation.

Employment Application Form

This form often replaces the need for the resume, but even then a resume might be accepted with it. Pay attention to data accuracy and completeness. When filled online, some systems will show when information is missing, and might not even allow the applicant to proceed to other sections.

—— Conviction History Form

Normally this is a brief form with very few questions. However, read it carefully to make sure your answers are done correctly. This will help avoid any future consequences.

—— MLIS Transcripts

Few libraries request the inclusion of the complete transcript of the Master in Library and Information Science degree. It is usually required as part of the application package by academic libraries. Other libraries might require it to be presented at the hiring phase. It is not unheard of that all college transcripts must be submitted too.

—— Driver License

Libraries in some states request the applicant's driver's license number and it can also be part of the position requirement. Regardless of the reason, it is a very common requirement at many libraries' application forms. In the case of Extra-Help Librarians covering more than one library—which can result in a lot of driving- it really justifies requiring the document.

—— Demographics Information Sheet

This is an Equal Employment Opportunity form which helps compile statistical data on race, ethnicity, and demographics. Its submission is optional and an individual's data is kept confidential.

—— Supplementary Questionnaire

This questionnaire is often part of the list of documents to be submitted online. It contains a variety of questions on professional skills and experiences. It can also be a couple questions that require more in dept responses about a scenario or professional issues.

Application Acceptance & Rejection Notification

In today's fast paced communication era, application notifications are no longer standardized, varying by institution. Job application by mail is no longer as common anymore and it has become rare for institutions to inform applicants that their application package was received. E-mail submission is not as reliable, since not all of them are sent to a specific contact person but to a department instead. This can make it more difficult to track delivery. The most efficient response method is the online submission. Shortly after the application is submitted, it emits an automatic e-mail confirming the receipt of it and some systems even allow applicants to follow the steps of the applicant's consideration process. Consequently, electronic applications eliminate some anxiety related to parts of the submission of job application.

In academic libraries it is not unusual for the hiring process to take months and communication can be delayed until the final decision is made. Other library types usually have a speedier selection process. Overall, in a tight library job marketplace, where there are more applicants than job openings, many rejection letters are not sent to those that did not qualify for the next step of the selection process: the interview. Such notifications can take a while to reach applicants due to a lengthy selection process, staff reduction and procedures simplification. Note that fewer personalized rejection letters are sent to applicants and often normal courtesies are dropped and no contact is ever made with an applicant. Electronic rejection letters are usually composed in a format that is computer reproduced to each applicant.

INTERVIEW PLANNING

Especially in a competitive market, it is a considerable achievement to reach the interview phase of an employment selection process. The communication of acceptance for interview is usually done by telephone and the date for the interview and or presentation is confirmed. During the interview preparation it is advisable to learn more about the library. Continue the research done when gathering information to create the cover letter that is attached to the job application. Now is the time to prove which applicant is the right choice for the position. More detailed information about the library, questions to be raised, and presentation preparation are some of the points listed below which can be further researched through the library website, Human Resources Department/Academic Affairs, staff, ALA reports and other educational sources.

- Library mission
- Funding sources
- Professional development
- Advancement opportunities
- Co-workers relations
- Union membership
- Hiring process
- Professional organization involvement
- Short and long term goals
- Leadership opportunities

Interviews usually involve a group decision and the interviewing board can be composed of people from different areas of the library such as appointed staff, supervisors, management representatives, etc. The board composition differs depending on the type of library and position. Extra-Help Librarian position interviews in public libraries will include a manager, position supervisor, and a human resources representative, for instance. In academic libraries—if the position involves instruction—reference and instruction supervisors and librarians will participate in the interview, evaluation, and selection.

Interview Types & Tips

In essence there are two types of interviews:

- Telephone or conference calls
- In-person interview

Academic libraries in particular have used telephone interviews as one of the first steps in the screening of candidates. In more recent years a variety of other libraries have used this method due to budgetary constraints. Funds to pay for candidates' transportation and hotel accommodations are not as available. Therefore, qualified out-of-area candidates are more likely to absorb their own expense. The in-person interview usually combines a candidate and the searching committee at academic libraries or the interviewing committees as it is known in public libraries.

Both scenarios are incorporating new technologies in the interactions between candidates and interviewers. Telephone interviews are adding more interviewers' participation, morphing into conference calls, some even with video capabilities. In-person interviews requiring presentations expect candidates to integrate the use of software in their showcase, demonstrating abilities often needed on the job. When using handouts, print more than you think you need and have the original a second copy handy for additional copies or to offer it to the board as a sample. When making presentations, practice and time it; store it as an email attachment or in a flash drive. Choose an appropriate format: plain text, pdf, or web; get informed about equipment (Mac, PC, teleconferencing medium, computer ports and other devices); and have a contingency plan if equipment fails or it is incompatible.

Regardless of the type of interview, prepare for it, relax, and show confidence. Remember that the process revolves around the applicant, the position, and the institution's evaluators. Express strong interest in the position, show how personal education and professional experience will be valuable, and ask fact-based questions related to the institution and position goals. In academic libraries, student population and library courses can serve as important observation points. In public libraries, customer service is highly demanding and a school library's support of curriculum is a topic that can be explored with interviewers. Generally, interviewers focus on candidate qualifications (experience and expertise), personality and performance (initiative, professional development, and future goals), body language (smile, eye contact, etc.) to choose the best potential contributor to the job and best fit for the institution's culture.

There is an abundance of resources on interviewing strategies in print and scattered over the World Wide Web. Lots of information on librarian position interviews and links to other sources can be accessed through http://mrlibrarydude.wordpress.com/nailing-the-library-interview/.

EMPLOYMENT CONSIDERATIONS

WAGES

Personnel regulations regarding Extra-Help Librarians focus on the specific nature of the category, such as irregular need, qualifications for benefits and budget allocations. Extra-Help Librarians' incomes are based on hourly wages and they fluctuate depending on work frequency. It can also happen that permanent part-time librarians can earn extra income with additional hours paid from the Extra-Help budget. Overall, a wide variation of wages is found nationwide (Miller, 2011; Eberts, 2009), following a similar pattern of librarian salaries, which depends on factors such as:

- Library type, size and location
- Permanent Part-Time or On-Call status
- Entry level
- Experience
- Specialization
- Foreign language skills
- Benefits
- Labor Unions

There is little room for negotiation. However, field specialization (business, medical) and foreign language skills might contribute to wage negotiation increase within the library pre-set wage range for this category. For instance, depending on the population diversity, some libraries make efforts to recruit bilingual personnel, especially librarians that interact face-to-face with patrons or do catalogue work.

The salary is issued whichever way the institution pays the other employees. Some job postings list the wages paid per hour, others don't, and a few treat it as a salary—for example when Extra-Help Librarians work in longer assignments of a few weeks or even a year. It depends also on how a personnel department classifies the position. Library Journal annually releases a salary survey (http://lj.libraryjournal.com/2012/10/placements-and-salaries/2012-survey/explore-all-the-data/) that gives librarians a measure of salaries countrywide. But it does not reflect any Extra-Help Librarian earnings. A research sample of Extra-Help Librarians job postings produced the following table that illustrates wages paid by various libraries in different states. The year listed refer to the date when the job was posted.

Wage By Hour	Library Type	State	Year
$ 15.31	Public – District	IL	2012
$ 17.45	Public – County	WA	2011
$ 20.00	Academic – College	IL	2012
$ 22.60	Public – County	MD	2012
$ 23.18	Public – City	ME	2012
$ 28.02	Public – City	NY	2010
$ 43.16	Academic – Community College	CA	2012
Wage Per Day	Academic - Community College	State	Year
$ 125.00	School – District	IL	2011
$ 116.00 + bonus	School – District	CA	2011

Table No. 1.2 Wage Samples

Even though it can be misleading, a quick way to obtain estimated earnings for Extra-Help Librarians is to use the keyword "Extra-Help Librarian" to search the Simplyhired website (http://www.simplyhired.com/a/salary/home). It provides features to calculate earnings per position in a city or state. The average changes when searching by state and a specific city. For example, in California the average for an Extra-Help Librarian is $46,000, but in San Francisco it is $56,000. This data is relevant for estimation, but in reality the category's earnings are also subject to other fluctuations, depending on the needs of the institution and a worker's availability. A factor such as the rise or fall of sick time requested by full-time or part-time librarians each year radically influences the total earnings of Extra-Help Librarians. On the same note, if they are sick themselves or unavailable for any other reason, they work less and the income will be reduced.

Another issue related to wages is the fact that Extra-Help Librarians are not necessarily locked into the entry level position pay rate. Recent graduates and others without librarian experience normally get the entry level pay rates. However, professionals with desirable track record as a librarian might be hired into a higher category and consequently at a higher per hour pay rate. Retired librarians, in particular those coming from the same institution ranks, are most likely able to earn higher pay rates. These cases are exceptions, but they demonstrate that it is possible for Extra-Help Librarians to obtain earnings at a higher level than the entry level rates generally listed on job postings.

Pay Rate Regulators

Extra-Help Librarians pay increases and changes in category (Librarian I, II) are interrelated because they affect pay rates. These factors are regulated differently by each library following labor laws or union agreements. Pay increase is treated generally as a direct consequence of the annual inflation percentage. In good years, when the library has no funding problems, the inflation percentage is applied and the pay rate will increase automatically—unless there is a clause in the employment agreement that states otherwise.

The total number of hours worked per fiscal year is also used as a benchmark, leading to increases in pay rates and even a change in job category. Limits are set for the total number of hours Extra-Help Librarians are allowed to work in a fiscal year. Libraries have set totals that vary, usually between 700–1200 hours or less. The number of hours worked within a year is carefully tracked by the Personnel Department/Human Resources to avoid overtime payment and change in job category which can result in more expenses for the library. This can ultimately affect the budget. Any limit of the yearly work hours might be mentioned in job interviews or in the hiring phase. It is an important factor that job applicants should be aware of because it really affects their potential earnings.

ORGANIZATIONAL CHART PLACEMENT

Employees are interconnected in relation to job responsibilities, including decision making and collaboration, and organizational charts are used to illustrate it. Extra-Help Librarians benefit from such tool in two instances, before and after they are hired. During the job search, or even at the hiring process phase, it allows job applicants to learn about the library structure and where they would fit in. If the institution does not have an official organizational chart, it is appropriate to ask about the supervision levels or categories which relate to the position. During the life of their employment, Extra-Help Librarians would have a clear view of their placement in the organization. This can facilitate communication amongst their main supervisor, project managers, and other staff they work with frequently or occasionally.

In practice, even the chain of command for Extra-Help Librarians changes constantly. It can be confusing to determine who they respond to because they work in different projects, departments or units and under various staff supervisors. Serving adult, youth, and children's services, involving reference, instruction and even technical services, can present challenges in positioning Extra-Help Librarians in an organizational chart. However, a library's organizational chart clarifies who has direct powers and responsibilities over them. Without this fundamental tool, institutions and workers lack understanding of the chain of command, leaving space for miscommunication in a variety of situations, from mere routine to emergencies and especially when personnel or procedural problems arise. Then, a library's placement of Extra-Help Librarians in the organizational chart may be a practical matter.

Furthermore, libraries usually do not differentiate permanent librarians from Extra-Help Librarians in their organizational chart since they are most likely in the same department. For example, the Seattle Public Library has both categories under Public Services. Other institutions combine them under general groups such as part-time librarians or even hourly librarians, making it more difficult to identify the category in organizational charts.

TRAINING & PROFESSIONAL DEVELOPMENT

Continuing learning is a necessity for librarians' professional life cycle. Efforts need to be made to stay current on career issues, ever changing collections, and library procedures. Once hired the employee orientation and job training takes place. This orientation phase introduces the organization and specific departments. The library's personnel policies handbook or employee handbook are handed out, stating specific terms and conditions of employment, including applicable laws, employment policies, benefits, behavior guidelines and other applicable standards. Subsequently, duties and responsibilities are learned along with various procedures.

Even though employee orientation and training is crucial for Extra-Help Librarians, coaching and mentoring is also important in the long term. They provide support to individual employees in many areas and libraries that provide these assistance tools are more likely to improve performance and create more motivated, efficient, and productive employees. A higher quality service to patrons and increased staff growth, especially for new librarians, are some of the benefits that result from consistent training. It also increases employment desirability in these libraries.

Often in academic libraries the hiring process already determines which areas are in need of support in reference or instruction, among others. Consequently, Extra-Help Librarians might focus on more in-depth information in certain areas. Acquiring the information necessary to perform everyday tasks and the knowledge gained in the training sessions are even more valuable if the librarian is involved in new faculty training, student orientation, and any kind of presentation about the library. Such opportunities offer the most up-to-date information.

Extra-Help Librarians can benefit from the "Tips for New Librarians" (Howard, 2007) even though it is geared to school media specialists. The suggestions about rules and procedures, participation, promotion, familiarization with the collections and employee attitude fits in with the basics of training to succeed on the job. As time goes by, continuous education through participation in workshops and conferences are other options to sharpen skills and to increase chances to make employment transitions.

Over the course of employment, employee training is often continued with meetings for updates, in-house workshops where employees have a choice and chance to participate, and through courses promoted by outside organizations. Managers or supervisors verify professional development funds and whether the course is useful for library employees in order to approve attendance. Such opportunities might not be available to Extra-Help Librarians, depending on the availability of budgeted funds for such purposes and a library's recognition of the category need for professional development.

In general, in-house training is often directed toward improving basic tasks related to technology updates and customer service skills, to cite a few common purposes. Some libraries are quite large and well funded, affording outside speakers and instructors. Also, in some cases they even have their own in-house training department. Other professional development alternatives, for free or for a fee, are available through WebJunction (www.webjunction.org), Infopeople (http://infopeople.org), Association of Colleges and Research Libraries—ACRL (http://www.ala.org/acrl/), and other professional organizations.

SCHEDULE MANAGEMENT

Scheduling Options

The distribution of work amongst the Extra-Help Librarians can be done by a designated employee, such as a schedule coordinator, or electronically and, to a certain degree, a combination of both. The chosen way to make such distribution depends on the size and needs of the library. Small libraries handle absences more easily since they have fewer employees. Participants in the extra-help pool might receive sporadic calls to work one day or get long-term assignments set in advance. Libraries that are big or are part of a library system have a large number of librarians. Therefore, it is much more complex to fill absences, especially in the cases of long-term needs for Extra-Help Librarians. A coordinator or the Human Resources Department, combined with a unit supervisor or branch manager, is usually responsible for temporarily filling the position.

Assignment distribution involves factors such as the Extra-Help Librarian availability, quantity of jobs, date, and location. Matching this information with the needs of the library requires clear procedures to maximize results. To better understand job distribution systems, the focus here will be on two systems—paper and automated—and will cover the steps in each process. However, note that the processes described here are not done the same way in each library type. Structural differences are reflected in the procedures, but the relevance of the systems is unquestionable.

Paper System

In the organizational structure of the library there may be an Extra-Help coordinator, or equivalent position, with the responsibility to manage the work distribution. In other cases there may just be a staff member who takes on this task amongst many others. For instance, it can be delegated to a volunteer coordinator, or another staff member who has high organizational skills, regardless of their job description.

The paper system, utilizing a scheduling coordinator, has been around for a long time and it is still a common system in place to fulfill libraries vacancy needs. As far as the processing of requests for Extra-Help Librarians, it starts with a request, either verbal or by a form, from the branch manager stating the need for staff coverage at specific dates and times.

Types of requests:
- Immediate need
- Advanced planning

Immediate requests include same day coverage for sudden absences, such as illness or personal emergencies. This request does not require the submission of a paper form. If the manager receives notification of absence before the library staff working hours, they might call an Extra-Help Librarian directly. In case this attempt is not successful, the Extra-Help coordinator is notified and will take over and make more contacts to obtain coverage.

Planned requests are predictable since they are scheduled in advance. Examples of this type might be medical appointments, surgeries, pregnancy leave, vacations, meetings, professional conferences, training, outreach, job vacancy or sabbaticals. This request type demonstrates common steps used in the paper system. Once the Extra-Help Librarians request form is sent by the manager to the coordinator, they would match the request with the Extra-Help Librarian's availability and try to divide the amount of jobs equally amongst the pool.

There are several factors to be considered when dividing job assignments. Some of them are the Extra-Help Librarian's availability (dates, times, vacations, shifts and other assignments), branch location, and even the employee and the manager/supervisor's preference. Job distribution is also effected by reliable information from the employee. Any mismatches are reduced to a minimum when their data is current. The update of an Extra-Help Librarian's schedule is an individual's important responsibility. When a coordinator is working on job distribution, they assume that a substitute's calendar reflects current availability. Procedures generally say that if there is a change in availability it should be communicated to the coordinator. Otherwise, this omission can reflect on the employee's reliability and any delivery of future assignments. An outdated schedule is detrimental to the Extra-Help Librarian and also wastes coordinator's time. The way schedules are updated can be as simple as using a monthly calendar page which is sent to Extra-Help Librarians and they can make the necessary notes on the days and hours that they would be open to take assignments.

Scheduling takes time to get finalized, requiring notifications by telephone and e-mail. These common forms of contact, announce the needs of staff replacement on specific dates, times and location. Usually responses are fast. If not, follow up call is made to the Extra-Help Librarian to obtain a confirmation or rejection of a job. Depending on the reply, new strategies may be necessary. The process was more difficult when there weren't answering machines, cell phones, and other quick means of communication.

Future jobs might be settled weeks in advance and may be divide more equally. Last minute assignments are not as equally divided because short term needs have to be met. At that point, the Extra-Help Librarians who is more readily available or able to respond more quickly has increased chances to get the days' work. There is no wait time for multiple responses to share the distribution of same day requests for employee replacement.

Short notice job vacancies can be problematic to fill but long term assignments can be even more complicated. There are many Extra-Help Librarians who are not available for long periods of time. Consequently, these jobs are often taken by a few in the category's pool, perhaps infringing the equality of opportunity and at times even raising questions about favoritism. In such circumstances, it can possibly represent an unfair job distribution. After the allocation of the open assignments is done, the Extra-Help coordinator sends the form back to the branch with the information about which Extra-Help Librarian will cover an absence and on which specific days and times.

In general, it is common procedure to fill the requests for the central or main library first and then the branches, unless the coverage is done separately by different coordinators. This illustrates how the paper system provides more control of absence coverage by location and even by personnel, as previously discussed.

Automated System

Online scheduling provides an interface with two access points:

- Administration: scheduler or manager
- Extra-Help

Automated scheduling systems allow library managers to enter requests for substitutes directly into the system, they allow Extra-Help Librarians to "search for jobs" at their convenience, and a payroll department to track substitute's hours and compensation more easily. Other advantages are related to cutting costs, minimizing errors, and making personnel adjustments easier. Overall, it is efficient, quick and easy.

In a decentralized organization, administrators or library managers hold most of the responsibility to input the jobs into the system. The data fields includes dates, time, location, name of the absent employee, job number, and notes. When the information is entered, it is released for viewing by all available Extra-Help Librarians. That is the premise, but in reality the first one that sees it can accept it, or not. Another option managers have is to pre-arrange jobs for a specific Extra-Help Librarian. This is discouraged to keep it fair to all members of the pool, giving them an equal chance to access assignments.

When administration opts for such a system it transfers more responsibilities to Extra-Help Librarians since they have to directly maintain their availability and frequently search for jobs. Even though the nature of the position can be insecure and unsteady, online scheduling adds to the challenges. Constant checking for jobs offers more chances of obtaining them, but it is time-consuming and tiresome. It's a random approach and the pressure is on Extra-Help Librarians, since if they don't check the system they will not be able to get work. Also, competition for jobs amongst Extra-Help Librarians can not be ignored. There are times when the jobs are fewer and sparser due to budget cuts and less scheduled vacations, for example. Conditions of this nature will make it even more difficult to obtain assignments. In addition, securing frequent work often depends on how technology savvy the Extra-Help Librarian is and what kind of gadgets (telephone or computer types) are used to access the system. Consequently, it can require much more effort to secure an assignment.

Some argue that the advantages are considerable. It takes the middle-man and subjectivity out of scheduling. The opportunities are available to all Extra-Help Librarians interested in getting as much work as they want or can get from the system. Having the time and the tools to access it is fundamental. The system is accessible 24/7 from anywhere, as long as there is a way to connect to it.

The system sends out job cancellation notices. Last minute changes are rare and they are handled by the job location administrator. Long-term assignments are not usually offered through the automated system. Generally, the Human Resources Department notifies Extra-Help Librarians via e-mail, for instance. Once the schedule is pre-arranged it is then added to the system.

Employee Scheduling Software

Various substitute schedule management systems are available, offering features that facilitate entry of information by the employer and easy access to jobs by employees. Some of the systems in the market are:

- SubFinder   http://www.crsadvancedtechnology.com/products/subfinder
- Aesop   http://www.aesopeducation.com/#1
- Callplus+   http://www.trasoft.net/callplus.asp
- Sub-IT   http://www.centralxchange.com/
- TeamWork   http://www.schedulesource.com/Employee-Scheduling.aspx

We will focus on SubFinder due to our experience with it. This system staffs employee absences and it is also widely used by schools, managing substitute teachers. For example, the Los Angeles Unified School District detailed instructions on connecting to SubFinder through the telephone (http://www.teachinla.com/substitute/subfinder_substitute.html) and this facilitates the understanding of how it works. SubFinder Online is another access option which is used by many organizations and a tutorial is available at http://www.crsadvancedtechnology.com/substitute/. These options are often inclusive and organizations' employees can utilize both, making it more convenient for job seekers, Extra-Help Librarians pool members in this case. There a need to use a telephone or computer to connect to the system frequently to find assignments available. The system matches the employee availability with the assignments' days, times, and location. Verify the details of the job(s), accept if interested or ignore it, proceeding to log out.

Once signed in the online screen shows the name of the employee (Extra-Help Librarian), available jobs, current jobs, personal information (including availability), do not disturb/unavailable, and tutorial. There is an available jobs page where future jobs are on top, followed by those already past. Other details such as job number, absent employee or purpose, location, and date/time/duration are also featured. Once an Extra-Help Librarian accepts a job it is consequently added to the list of future assignments. Changes occur frequently in these screens since jobs are posted daily, depending a library's size and needs.

Time Management

There are many different ways and preferences on how to keep track of the Extra-Help Librarian's assignments. Print and electronic calendars are the common types used to maintain work dates. The choice is a matter of preference, but make it accessible at all times to avoid confusion and mistakes. Even the most organized Extra-Help Librarian at some point may happen to get to the wrong location, date and times. Acceptance and a sense of humor help in such occasions and you should take the occurrence as a learning experience. Embarrassment apart, staff realize how difficult it is to Extra-Help Librarians to keep schedule mistake free all the time.

It is demanding to keep control of assignment dates and also to search for upcoming jobs. Organization and persistence are key elements in obtaining work through the online system. The paper system is handled by a coordinator and Extra-Help Librarians have a more passive role in obtaining work. So, last minute calls to fill same day absences is a very challenging assignment and hard to accommodate into Extra-Help Librarians personal lifestyle. It takes a malleable mind to make the adjustment and yet many people seem to thrive in such circumstances. Flexibility and commitment to the position are essential to combine a personal life and a library's staff needs.

Cancellations

Occasional cancellation of assignments by the organization or Extra-Help Librarians happens sooner or later due to unpredictable circumstances or mistakes. Cancellation procedures establish responsibilities for both parties. For example, how far in advance libraries can make cancellations without having to pay for Extra-Help Librarians' time or who should notify them after a cancellation is done online are issues that need to be clearly addressed. Information of this nature helps increase schedule accuracy and minimize misunderstandings. Extra-Help Librarian's reliability is crucial in their position and supervisors always appreciate advanced notice of changes.

WORK ETHICS

Professional commitment involves the incorporation and defense of values which are stated in ALA's Code of Ethics (http://www.ala.org/advocacy/proethics/codeofethics/codeethics). Principles such as intellectual freedom, right to privacy and confidentiality, intellectual property rights, respect, fairness, level of service and professional development, serve as a guide to librarians when managing their responsibilities. As well, they can secure the rights of patrons and other employees. Even though their decision-making is limited, Extra-Help Librarian's observance of the ALA statements can guide them in handling conflicts or disputes. It can govern how to report them to the librarian in charge for future follow up. However, Extra-Help Librarians' ethics also extend to practical points. Some of them include the following:

Promptness

Punctuality and promptness are relevant aspects in any Extra-Help Librarian's work conduct. These qualities generate patrons, colleagues, and administrators goodwill. Staff and supervisors in particular are attentive of Extra-Help behavior and their conformity to standards and rules. Such considerations are relevant to note because performance evaluations and word-of-mouth influence future job availability and placements. Regular staff at times can resent the Extra-Help Librarian position. Sometimes it is easier to overlook the inherent disadvantages and the work flexibility can be envied, for instance. It is important to avoid coming to work late, stretching breaks and mealtime and leaving earlier than scheduled. These actions can be interpreted as privileges and they are hard to ignore. It is best to be part of the organization, showing commitment and respect while being on time and willingly doing the assigned work.

Procrastination

Extra-Help Librarians have no time for procrastination due to their strict schedule at one or more locations. They are scheduled for short assignments, a day or a week, for instance, and often there is not much time to get projects accomplished. There might not be a chance to continue the work the next day because they could well be someplace else. Frequently, work delegated to them has no immediate deadline and can be continued by others. However, if it is not a necessity, it is a courtesy to notify local staff about the status of projects since it facilitates the continuation of the tasks. The basic rule is to do it here and now to lessen the need for the permanent staff to follow up.

Confidentiality

No doubt patrons' records are one of a library's major confidentiality issues. Also, there are other workplace matters that need to be treated carefully. Extra-Help Librarians are specially exposed to sensitive comments to and from the regular staff. The infrequency with which they relate to those in a branch or campus can make them seem to be trusting listeners. They are not immersed in routine conflicts and they are not likely to share the information with others in the same location. On the other hand, they can—unintentionally or not—convey what they experienced to other locations. Therefore, a Extra-Help Librarian's discretion plays an important part regarding the confidentiality issues of colleagues in various locations. The professional's awareness about information sharing requires astute judgment of what they hear to avoid breaching confidentiality and trust.

STRESS

Changes can generate fear and anxiety and each person manages it differently. Extra-Help Librarians confront many changes on a regular basis and they need to understand their own needs and responsibilities, as well as the requirements of the position to regulate their levels of stress. Evaluation of how many hours of work and income amount they need or want, the distance they are willing to commute, and the level of responsibilities they want to take prepare them in advance for some of the issues they will occur. Also, when starting a new job, serving one or more locations, learning the routine, getting to know the collection and their arrangement in each building are reasons for anxiety. Usually, over time self-confidence increases and stress tends to decrease.

Each Extra-Help Librarian group, retirees, transitioners and new librarians, has distinct goals and needs which influences their emotional balance. Retirees tend to have a better handling of the matter than other groups, perhaps due to their relative stable finances and professional experience. Transitioners with dependents struggle to balance the need of others with their personal and professional life. A challenging schedule can generate increased efforts and tensions. New librarians—without previous experience in a library environment—might confront unpredictable situations with less ease and increased anxiety.

In addition, there are many other situations which trigger Extra-Help Librarian's stress:

- Keeping track of schedules
- Seeking assignments

- Driving/commuting to various libraries
- Confronting problems with patrons
- Reorienting themselves frequently
- Lack of communication in the library or system

Extra-Help Librarians are not immune to stress and learning about the reasons that trigger restlessness—especially in the workplace—is a way to handle situations in a more positive manner. For instance, the continuing rotation from one location to another, here today and tomorrow at someplace else, can act as stress release or can act as stress increase. Some individuals welcome new challenges as a learning opportunity, while others have a difficult time handling such situations. Assessment of personal abilities and comfort levels in fluid environments are indicators of how well an individual fits in an Extra-Help Librarian position. Awareness of external and internal factors that generate stress can lead to the identification of possible ways to handle them, even though there are many different concerns and stress zones. Extra-Help Librarians share some of the same issues that regular staff confronts, including daily difficulties, a library's reduction of hours or closure, corroding moral, and lay-offs. They suffer pressure from many angles and if not kept in control it can affect work performance. In essence, administrators need to consider the Extra-Help Librarians stress points—and their impacts—to maintain a well-balanced workforce.

LIBRARY OPEN HOURS

Type, location and a budget's healthiness will influence the determination of how long libraries stay open. For example, a metropolitan public library will keep its doors open weekdays, weekends and evening hours, but their branches are more likely to suffer reduction in hours. Traditionally an academic and school library's open hours follow the school year schedule. Academic libraries close or reduce their hours drastically between semesters, and maintain long hours when school is in session. School libraries usually keep the same hours as the school administration and teachers. This means an early start, consistent closure time, school breaks and less evening and weekend hours.

Therefore, when considering a job, it is advantageous to know the library's open hour cycles to evaluate potential work throughout the year. Availability on evenings and weekends can increase the chances to get more assignments, since permanent staff often wants to take time off then. Part-time staff is frequently hired specifically to cover these less desirable hours. Schedule rotation is another aspect to take in account since staff's personal commitments might conflict with their work schedule. This will generate more need for Extra-Help Librarians. A librarian's use of compensation time can be a source of more work as well.

During short assignments, Extra-Help professionals starting time and working hours vary. Normally they start when the library opens and they are scheduled for fewer hours—unless they are covering a permanent staff person that has library opening or set up responsibilities. Short assignments last a few hours (some libraries offer a minimum per day) or all day, depending on management determination of needs. Long assignments are set in advance. Even though they are subject to changes during its course, there is less possibility of fluctuations.

In recent years newspapers and professional magazines have frequently reported on the shrinkage of library hours. Administration makes efforts to cope with such challenges along with staff reorganization. In such context, the need for Extra-Help Librarians is also re-evaluated. But it tends to continue as a viable alternative to maintain an adequate level of public services.

PERFORMANCE EVALUATION

It is not uncommon to perceive evaluation as a threat, fearing changes in the status quo. However, lots of positive insights result from it. Performance evaluation, used as a form of communication between library administration and staff, generates feedback on the institution and employee. It is to everyone's benefit to review the services provided and the employee's contribution to work quality.

Like other employees, Extra-Help Librarians participation in performance evaluation processes is also necessary. It might not be as straight forward because of the complexities involved. Extra-Help Librarians work in various locations and with many staff persons and may require specific evaluation methods to measure their performance. Administrators might designate one supervisor to gather the needed information—from unit managers in other work sites, perhaps—for the performance interview. Exact position characteristics, which include a wide range of projects, make it more difficult to identify accomplishments and difficulties. Specific work standards and expectations guidelines should be used in the evaluation of a Extra-Help Librarian's performance.

Consistent employee evaluations helps take the stress out of the process. In the case of a Extra-Help Librarian's performance, frequent reviews take the surprise factor out of it. Aiming to avoid poor performance, it is advisable to connect with managers or coordinators to learn about the factors taken into the evaluation. Components such as work knowledge and delivery quality, attendance and punctuality, flexibility, time management and interpersonal skills (Dorio, 2011) are suitably incorporated in a Extra-Help Librarian's performance review.

Managers or supervisors who keep track of employee's accomplishments and challenges are more equipped to produce better evaluations. Employees who are responsible and attentive to procedures have fewer challenges in the evaluation process. In the case of Extra-Help Librarians under less direct supervision, they have more responsibilities to keep track of what they do, how well they do it and the outcomes. It is critical to maintain a certain level of self-evaluation, since at performance evaluation time there will be few people they work for or with to discuss merits and difficulties. The more Extra-Help Librarians are focused on the work expectations and their performance, the easier the evaluation process.

WORKERS RETENTION

Professional development, position responsibilities, wages/salary, benefits, work environment and relationship with colleagues, and mentoring (Stevens, 2003) are some important aspects for librarian retention, especially for new librarians in entry-level positions. As well, flexibility, work conditions and professional prospects encourage extra-help to stay in the pool. The fact that the position provides opportunities to get a regular staff position, part-time or full-time, also motivates them to perform well. Extra-Help Librarians in need of basic benefits, such as medical and dental, are more apt to explore job opportunities outside of their library or library system, especially if in-house openings are scarce.

New librarians and transitioners are possible candidates for job openings. They also tend to work more frequently and are more susceptible to changes in their employment status. Consequently, these two groups are the most likely to leave the extra-help pool. Retirees' interest continues to be on occasional short or month long term assignments. Considering these differences, further research is necessary to identify an applicable turn over rate.

Libraries in financial hardship unavoidably take measures which can reduce the Extra-Help Librarians pool. However, this category retention continues to be necessary. Basic library coverage of absences, vacations and other occurrences still require staff support. Cutting their budget generates minimal work, reducing their income drastically which can lead to low moral, lack of motivation or detachment from the library. Administration's open communication keeps professionals informed about the library's difficulties and decisions. Therefore, when Extra-Help Librarians are in the midst of such circumstances, they can be more understanding of priorities set by administration and more prone to stay on the job.

PROFESSIONAL ADVANCEMENT

Frequently libraries need to hire due to retirement, department transfers, promotions or other reasons. This offers new job openings and opportunities for advancement. Extra-Help Librarians often take advantage of staff mobility and apply for part-time or full-time positions. From an administrator's perspective, Extra-Help Librarian pools are resourceful, providing readily available workers to fulfill a library's immediate needs (e.g. staff absence, leaves, etc.) at reduced costs (less benefits, for instance). It is a source of trained professionals on reserve to fill vacancies. Pool participants on the other hand, in particular from the new librarians and transitioners groups, are especially interested in upcoming openings. Depending on the opportunity and timing, they might decide to apply for the position, seeking to change their category status. However, when Extra-Help Librarians know the institution too well, perhaps perceiving that the organizational culture does not fit their own values, they prefer not to commit to a position with more responsibilities. Decisions are based on many personal factors, but specifics about the opening—such as area (adult, young adult, children), location (main or branch) or community, as well as the manager/supervisor (supportive, engaged)—weighs heavily on their decisions.

Considering the characteristics of the job, an Extra-Help Librarian's skills allow for many professional opportunities. Continuing changes are taking place in libraries and in the profession, and this makes flexibility and adaptability essential skills in times of transition. Extra-Help Librarian's valuable crossover experience in many areas—such as in reference, instruction, technology and research areas—enhance employment prospects.

The position provides chances to increase professional confidence. This confidence can be acquired, for instance, confronting unexpected situations, responding quickly to staff and patrons' needs, meeting short deadlines or interacting with diverse communities. The skills obtained are transferable to other jobs in different types of libraries and other organizations. Prospective employers, seeking professionals with broader experience and willing to train for specific needs, encounter in an Extra-Help Librarian a professional with strong potential.

A collection of information about the economy and effect on the library is a primary step on job searches. These factors will indicate the current library status and future opportunities. In a declining economy, any library is undermined if communities are not committed to support it through difficulties. In a receding system, Extra-Help Librarians support efforts to maintain the level of service quality. They are not meant to replace regular staff, they are part of a support system which by its own purpose is not set up to be relied upon for long periods of time.

When a library budget is healthy, Extra-Help Librarian's benefits will be more readily provided. Benefits will continue to vary amongst organizations, but proportional benefits such as health and accrued sick leave are more likely to be offered. What attract librarians to this position varies depending on their age, goals, and employment needs. Future prospects depend on personal interests and an institution's economic stability.

BUDGET

Familiarity with the library's budget increases the understanding of their financial health. Libraries' websites often post their general budget to the public, stating income and expenditures, and other valuable information. A detailed budget at position levels is not usually available, but it is advisable to find out how positions fit in the expected expenses for the fiscal year. Depending on the type of budget, the estimated expenses for Extra-Help Librarians might be combined with other expenses. Without budget transparency it becomes difficult to have a clear comprehension of how it affects a particular professional category. In cases where there is a union representing staff's interest through contracts with library administration, detailed budget information is more readily available.

Ideally, workers should know more about how budgets impact their career but in reality it is often during financial crises that such concerns arise. When the economy is depressed organizations restructure themselves, seeking to trim expenses radically and libraries are no exception. In times of budget cuts more positions are dependent on availability of funds and extra-help will most likely be affected first before other staff members. This occurrence might be explicit in the personnel and union agreements, but it can also come suddenly and unexpectedly. Yet, the library's progressive loss of income indicates future impact on staffing.

During crisis, staff is pressured to take on more responsibilities and Extra-Help Librarian's hours tend to diminish. Special projects receive lower priority and extra-help categories can experience less demand. Supervisors will be more careful about requesting extra-help, delegating more responsibilities to regular staff, stretching as much as possible to provide basic needs. Consequently, Extra-Help Librarians will get less days than they used to and even the number of hours per day tend to decline. Even though they are still needed to cover vacations, sick leave, and last minute staff needs, the opportunities are scarcer. This is especially true when the pool size remains the same and there can be an increased competition for fewer jobs.

Cuts in personnel do not necessarily mean that Extra-Help Librarians will lose their jobs, since they earn per hour and do not have the benefits that full-time and regular part-time employees have. However, their wages can also be lowered when staff is suffering salary freezes. An important aspect to be inquisitive about is how permanent such retractions may be. Are these conditions temporary and bound to go back to where they were when a library income improves or are they more permanent and a future wage increase will be required?

Staffing maintenance is costly, and the obligations with an extra-help pool also requires payment of wages, pro-rated medical benefits in some institutions, additional workers compensation insurance, a coordinator salary or fee payment for automated scheduling system and other factors. Therefore, managers are careful to keep requests for Extra-Help Librarians low or to a minimum. Budget repercussions are far more important than most workers realize. Extra-Help Librarians' expectations are more realistic when they understand a library's funding sources, as well as administration's strategies and operating priorities. Clearly, there is no security for the category even when the budget is sound and the economy is going well. However, strategies to cope with such financial uncertainties involve setting personal and professional goals, including alternative workplaces.

UNION MEMBERSHIP

A relationship between libraries and unions create particular rights and responsibilities that effect employees. Libraries have many expenditures and staffing takes a high percentage of their income. It recognizes unions' duties to their members, but much debate exists while defending self interests. Unions' tenants are linked to the pursuit of suitable working conditions, fair salaries and wages, job security, health care, and other benefits. The membership options are as a fee paying member or as a full member who has voting rights. Even though Extra-Help Librarians do not get some of these major benefits, they are not exempt from making a monetary contribution to the union, even if they do not agree in being part of it. They are designated as fee members and the fee amount is taken directly from their earnings on a pay-period basis. The level of involvement of Extra-Help Librarians in unions as full members is a personal choice that may or may not be directly connected to the benefits that it can bring to individuals. There is much debate on the advantages and disadvantages of unions.

Updates on union news, negotiations, and more are presented from different angles and channels through union websites, blogs, chat groups, and the general media. Sources such as ALA Connect (http://connect.ala.org/node/71716) and Union Library Workers (http://unionlibraryworkers.blogspot.com/) provide discussion and frequent updates on issues of interest to libraries and other information professionals.

CHAPTER REFERENCES

Dorio, M. & Shelly, S. (2011). *The complete idiot's guide to boosting employee performance.* New York, NY: Penguin Group.

Eberts, M. & Gilser, M. (2009). *McGraw-Hill's careers for bookworms & other literary types* (4th ed.). New York, NY: McGraw-Hill. 69.

Howard, S. (2007). Tips for new librarians. In J. Repman & G. K. Dickinson (Eds.), *School Library Management* (6th ed.). Columbus, OH: Linworth Pub.

Jones, W. (2011). Re-engaging/engaging part-time librarians. *College & Undergraduate Libraries,* 18, 37-42.

Massis, B. (2008). The substitute librarian – providing a mechanism for the library learner to learn. In *The challenges to library learning: solutions for librarians.* New York, NY: Routledge.

McNeil, B. & Gieseck, J. (2001). *Core Competencies for Libraries and Library Staff. In staff development: a practical guide* (3rd ed.). E. F. Avery, T. Dahlin, & D. A. Carver (Eds.). American Library Association. Retrieved from http://archive.ala.org/editions/samplers/sampler_pdfs/avery.pdf

Miller, R. (2011). LJ 2011 *Job satisfaction survey: rocked by recession, buoyed by service.* Retrieved from http://www.libraryjournal.com/lj/careerscareernews/890617-300/lj_2011_job_satisfaction_survey.html.csp

Oliver, M. (2003, Jul 6). *Miriam Matthews, 97; pioneering L.A. librarian was an expert in Black History.* Retrieved from http://articles.latimes.com/2003/jul/06/local/me-matthews6

Rockler-Gladen, N. (2006). *Online class advantages and disadvantages.* Nov. Retrieved from http://suite101.com/article/online-college-courses-a9807

SJSU – SLIS. *Career Pathways.* Retrieved from http://slisweb.sjsu.edu/classes/careerpathways/index.htm

Stevens, J. & Streatfield, R. (2003). *Recruitment and retention.* SPEC Kit 276. Washington, DC: ARL. Retrieved from http://www.arl.org/bm~doc/spec276webbook.pdf

Thompson, S. (2009). *Core technology competencies for librarians and library staff: a LITA guide.* LITA Guides, 15. New York, NY: Neal-Schuman Publishers.

OVERVIEW OF LIBRARIES 2

Over the last few years reduction in funding has been a major hurdle for libraries, leading to fewer resources and even staff reduction. It has become more challenging for libraries to provide services to their communities. Also, they are no longer the only information provider. With the growth of the internet these institutions face strong competition and they have had to rethink their operations and the way librarians work. It has been progressively necessary to be critical about what libraries have to offer in this new scenario. Instead of competing with the internet, librarians are using it as a tool to innovate, making their organizations surpass the premise that they are becoming obsolete.

The library type and mission delineate librarians' work. Generally, they have been organizers, materials selectors, creative programmers and patron assistants. In addition to these, now librarians' roles demand more involvement with others within and outside of the library. Consequently, each library uses a variety of strategies to meet their community needs. Academic and school libraries continually reinforce collaboration with faculty to better support the curriculum. They design and create technology based resources to provide more interactive opportunities for students to obtain the information that they need through the library. Public libraries are increasingly more engaged in offering their patrons electronic options, diversifying the collections and changing their programs to maintain repeat patrons and attract others.

Similarities and differences amongst libraries will be grouped in this section to better understand librarians' responsibilities and provide a general idea of public, academic and school libraries specifically in the context of Extra-Help Librarians work. Their professional profile has been outlined in the previous chapter and at this point the focus is on three components. First, on the information deemed necessary to understand each library type. Second, comprehend permanent librarians' functions and the tools used in each setting. Third, weave the Extra-Help Librarian handling of some of those responsibilities when temporarily replacing a permanent librarian.

Library Mission, Vision & Strategic Plan

The library mission is an essential document that answers questions of the following nature:

Who is the library serving?

What geographic area does it aim to reach?

What community needs does it support?

The information in a mission statement serves as a guide to shape the library vision which delineates the commitment to achieve higher standards for the betterment of the community. These basics are used to create a strategic plan where the library sets goals, such as implementing or improving services over a period of time. Guidelines lay out administrative responsibilities and library employees aim to reach specific goals. Their performances lead them closer to or away from accomplishing the expected results. Extra-Help Librarians also contribute to outcomes. Therefore, they should try to learn about the organization, understand how it works and how they are connected to it. Like in any other job position, while conducting the everyday responsibilities it is easy to loose sight of the broader implications of the work. However, it is very important to be attentive to the library's overall goals. The three types of libraries in focus here interrelate in some areas. Their missions, for instance, indicate where the cross-over is apparent. Extra-Help Librarians are motivated to investigate this further if they have interest in working in more than one of these libraries.

Classification Systems

Library materials are organized predominantly by two major library classification systems used in different type of libraries. Public and school libraries generally use the numeral based Dewey Decimal System (DOC) and academic libraries use the alphabetic organization of the Library of Congress Classification (LCC). The function of library classification is to provide a system in which library materials are coded and organized according to subject. There are two major steps in library classification. The first step describes the item, or tells what the information contained in the item (book, serial, periodical, dvd, etc.) is about. The second step assigns a call number based on this information that acts as the book's address in the collection.

To further understand the relation between the DOC and LLC classification systems, a comparison is available at http://home.olemiss.edu/~tharry/LC/LCvsDDC.htmll, clarifying the close relationship of the classification systems which are used widely in the United

States libraries and abroad. There is also an open-source alternative in place, the Open Shelves Classification, based on bookstores' shelving organization. Some small libraries have implemented this system.

Each of the systems mentioned encounter challenges in arranging library collections. Mastering a library classification system makes it easier to locate materials. Extra-Help Librarians are often already versed in most classification systems, perhaps due to their experience as a patron, cataloguing classes or even previous work in different libraries. When starting on their first position, newly graduated librarians might be more dependent on the library catalog for some time until they learn the local collection.

Location & Layout

Patrons' needs influence the layout of a library and materials are located in particular areas to facilitate access. Collections, computers equipment and staff working areas are often reconfigured to accommodate space limitations, increase circulation or assist patrons better. Especially when Extra-Help Librarians work in multiple places it can be difficult for them to learn the exact location of materials in a library. Even when they become more experienced and familiar with the placement of a collection in determined areas, it can be challenging to stay current on the latest changes.

Each library or department has their own way of arranging materials, but consistency in procedures is the best guide—especially to Extra-Help Librarians. Managers or area supervisors should keep them informed about a materials new location. During same day assignments, such instructions should be communicated, preferably before the building opens to the public. Updates reduce uncertainty about a material's location and promote accurate guidance of patrons to desired areas. Direct communication amongst personnel eliminates potential mistakes and excuses due to a lack of information. Extra-Help Librarians providing seamless service to patrons are not subject to embarrassment and apologies to patrons.

Job Considerations

RESPONSIBILITIES

Librarians' work involves research, evaluation of sources, technology troubleshooting and administrative tasks. Considering that Extra-Help Librarians cover vast amounts of responsibilities in different places, it is of important to know tasks well and have clear instructions on deviations from the norm. Even when they are not working as a solo librarian it is necessary to learn about changes and new procedures in a particular location.

The procedures manual for a library contains valuable information that serves as a guide, particularly if there are any questions. In some libraries a binder holds useful content and it is critical to keep it current or otherwise it defeats its purpose. Having a designated employee responsible to update it and date revisions simplifies the task. Easy identification and accessibility are also important—easy to see and reach. It should be clearly labeled to make it visible from other desk reference materials.

Extra-Help Librarians should check for any of the latest changes in the handbook folder since they last worked at that location—main library, campus site or regional branch. Some examples of materials added to the handbook are:

- Policy and procedures
- Opening and closing procedures
- Emergency phones - police or fire department
- Emergency contact list - supervisor, director
- Branch or campus directory - locations and hours
- Staff directory - names, job position, phone numbers and extension
- Programs and events - Summer reading, book discussion groups
- Map of collections layout by library location
- Incident report forms
- Volunteer forms
- Literacy referrals list

Some of this information is also available in the library website and it is helpful to know how to locate it quickly. If that is the case, politely provide the answers to the patron and also mention where they can find it next time they need it, just in case the library is closed. Empowering others is also part of a librarian's responsibilities, regardless of their job position.

SERVICES & PRIORITIES

Assistance to patrons in many areas is one of the most important and frequent services that a reference librarian provides. Extra-Help Librarians' knowledge about administrative policies and common customer service procedures can guide them when responding to patrons' requests. Professional training, experience and supervisor communication are other sources of guidance. There might be libraries that set different customer service approaches, but unless it is otherwise stated, attending patrons face-to-face comes first in the priority list as noted ahead, followed by other responsibilities such as:

- Patron face-to-face contact
- Next patron in line
- Telephone requests
- E-mails and virtual reference
- Colleague requests
- Administrative tasks

In addition, such priorities are not fixed and they adapt as real situations occur, depending on circumstances at the time. For example, when it is really busy at the reference desk, the minimum that can be done is to tend to a patron as quickly as possible and at intervals acknowledge the other patrons that are waiting. Use body language, making eye contact, smiling, expressing that you or a colleague will help them as soon as possible. It can happen that right in the middle of a transaction another patron will call on the telephone. Show promptness, clarity, and politeness. While the telephone patron waits, perhaps another librarian will be able to take the call sooner. In many cases, Extra-Help Librarians have the advantage of not differentiating a frequent from an occasional caller, making it easier to prioritize in an unbiased manner. Public libraries in particular have regular callers who need help placing requests or just want to check on the day's news. An Extra-Help Librarian's experience in different locations—working with various managers, staff and patrons—and their responsibility for a variety of tasks, requires effective skills. In addition, guidelines for behavioral performance from the Reference and User Services Association—RUSA (http://www.ala.org/rusa/resources/guidelines/guidelinesbehavioral) also serve as a support tool to the professional's experience.

ASSIGNED PROJECTS

On and off desk, there are many projects that Extra-Help Librarians are involved with on a regular basis. The nature, length and priority of the activities and projects vary by each location, library type and size. Priorities are set by the manager or supervisor and delegated on short notice to the incoming staff replacement. Both professionals show quick response to immediate needs, selecting and delegating on one hand, adapting and accomplishing tasks by the other. Often there is not a list of work that is reserved for Extra-Help Librarians, but common work that needs to be done. It might include:

- Discard processing and disposition of materials
- Materials lists (Hold/request, lost/missing lists)
- Shelf reading and displays
- Read trade publications for materials selection
- Archives support

- Data collection
- Research on specific subjects
- Bibliography annotations
- Gather information for subject guides

These are samples of what to expect, but there are many areas in which Extra-Help Librarians support other staff. In reality no limit is set on how challenging projects can be and there are no set standards on the level of professional skills required to do them. Work is not necessarily tied to assignment difficulty level, but on current library needs. At times these professionals wonder if they really needed to earn a Masters degree to do what is assigned to them. Understand that regardless of how simple or complex the work is, Extra-Help Librarians' contributions are normally directed to accomplish the library most pressing needs.

COLLECTION DEVELOPMENT

The library's collection development policy is a primary source for those interested in understanding the guidelines used to maintain and expand materials. Each institution creates its own policy considering their community needs, current collection and goals, physical space, staff and budget allocation. They can be elaborate, depending on the complexity of the institution, often by subject area or departmental areas. There are those that choose simpler guidelines. ALA provides guidance and samples on collection development (http://wikis.ala.org/professionaltips/index.php?title=Collection_Policies) and here are a few more examples:

- Cornell University Library
  http://www.library.cornell.edu/colldev/cdhome1.html
- Kenyon College, Gambior, Ohio
  https://lbis.kenyon.edu/colldev/
- Campbell County Public Library System
  http://ccpls.org/coldev/
- Morton Grove Public Library
  http://www.webrary.org/inside/colldevtoc.html
- Fargo Public Library
  http://www.cityoffargo.com/CityInfo/Departments/Library/AbouttheLibrary/PoliciesandProcedures/CollectionDevelopment-GeneralSelectionCriteriaanTools.aspx

Collection development is critical to libraries. Trained professionals and even whole departments are in charge of some or all steps of this process. A Extra-Help Librarian's participation in collection development varies depending on their subject area knowledge, assignment length, an institution's degree of collection centralization, departmental needs and acquisition deadlines. It is a time-consuming process and responsibilities consist of reading reviews of books and media materials, as well as checking new publications, revised editions and replacements for purchase against allocated funds. Familiarity with materials' review publications is also helpful to support staff needs in this area.

MATERIALS REVIEW TOOLS

Some reviewing publications focus on materials for specific library types and others offer reviews of a wide variety of materials that could fulfill the needs of patrons of any type of library. Reviews are generally concise and objective, and recommendations can be especially helpful. It is useful to be familiar with reviewing publications in their print and online version. Some of the publications that provide trustworthy materials reviews for collection development are:

- Choice Magazine or Choice Reviews Online
- Library Journal
- School Library Journal—Curriculum Connections
- Booklist
- Publisher's Weekly
- Kirkus Reviews
- Horn Books
- Serials Librarian

Library vendors such as Scholastitc and Baker & Taylor, might also provide their own review of the materials that they offer for purchase. Also, customer reviews from commercial websites can be questionable, but they can serve as a popularity gauge against other reviews.

SELECTION

Managers delegate limited selection responsibilities to Extra-Help Librarians, but opportunities arise, mostly during long assignments. Selection of specific formats, such as media or a section of the classification system, is a possibility. In addition, they often help in the process even though they might not have the opportunity to do the actual ordering. In any case, it is recommended to learn the basic aspects of selecting and ordering materials. Selection considerations involve the following aspects:

- Patrons interests and needs
- Collection needs and how it fits in the collection
- Content
- Purpose
- Price and budget
- Publication date
- Reviews

These factors influence public, school and academic libraries collections, reflection on their overall purchase. Materials content and formats differ due to the specificities of each library. For instance, some libraries emphasize fiction over non-fiction or dvd's over paperbacks. However, sometimes the same format can be found in all types of libraries. The table below shows some formats that are more common in certain libraries and others that can be available at any of them:

Public & School Libraries	Public Libraries	Public, Academic & School Libraries	Academic Libraries
• Picture books • Counting, Alphabet and Concept books • Easy Readers • First Chapters • Graphic Novels • Fiction and Non-Fiction • Books on CD's or cassettes • Non-English collections	• CD's and DVD's • Government documents • Microfiche, microfilm	• Maps • Braille books • Periodicals • E-collection books • E-Collection, books, music, lectures • Biographies, anthologies or story collections • Historical resources • Oversize books	• Thesis, monographs • Fiction and non-fiction for academic purpose • Microfiche, microfilm

Table No. 2.1. Collections & Formats by Library Type

When patrons need an item that is not available in their library, or in a specific format, they can be obtained through other means, including interlibrary loans. Extra-Help Librarians' knowledge of the options, the procedures and any possible fees contributes to patrons' well-informed decision-making.

NON-CIRCULATING MATERIALS

Materials for in library use only are labeled appropriately and the circulation system does not allow them to be checked out to patrons. Also, Extra-Help Librarians should be current on in-library use procedures for reference desk materials, if applicable. Often patrons are required to provide identification to use them. If working at the circulation desk, patrons unaware of these procedures might try to check-out non-circulating materials and they need to be informed about the check-out restriction of reference materials, magazines' latest issues and other items. For example, The Morton Grove Public Library (Brumley, 2006) states in its policies that the following reference materials are non-circulating:

Ready Reference Materials
Book or Periodical Indexes

Expensive Materials ($200+)
Frequently Used Materials
Multi-Volume Sets
Leased Items
Special collections
Reserve materials

TEST BOOKS & TEXTBOOKS

Public libraries usually do not acquire textbooks, even though there are some test books geared to GED, TOEFL, Civil Service preparation and other professional areas that require testing. Extra-Help Librarians should be aware of how these books are shelved. They may be kept separately with all the test books together or interfiled within the collection under their respective cataloging number. School libraries usually work alongside teachers to decide how to handle textbooks, either as part of the library collection or just in classroom collections. SAT test books and other examination books are also available. Academic libraries acquisitions of test books for graduate exams such as GMAT, teacher's credentials or other reasons often depend on departmental specialization and students' interests or requests. Librarians or department liaisons work with faculty to provide textbooks in reserve status at the circulation area under specific checkout rules, at times for library use only.

E - COLLECTION

Librarians in academic settings also focus on teaching students and faculty about digital books and textbooks, emphasizing issues that involve accessibility, information reliability and cost effectiveness of subscription and open source materials. Increasing e-book collections and departmental e-reserves, lead to the need to understand basic agreement points between the library and publishers in regards to requirements and restrictions. For example, students and faculty should be aware of costs and benefits, and restrictions on how many users are permitted to use the resource at once, to take advantage of the resources within the parameters of rights and responsibilities.

E-textbooks & E-books

The e-reserve services of academic libraries and school media centers make available e-textbooks and e-books to students. All types of libraries have specific concerns with this emerging technology since each one has its own set of standards and licensing arrangements. However, collection size, e-book prices, e-readers compatibility, accessibility, integration to catalog, and staff training (Waters, 2011) are aspects that libraries consider when investigating media platform options to make electronic collections available to their community. A partial list of e-textbooks and e-books publishers, e-readers devices and media platforms follows.

E-BOOKS & E-TEXTBOOKS PUBLISHERS:
- CA Free Digital Textbook Initiative   http://www.clrn.org/fdti/
- Courseload   http://www.courseload.com/
- CourseSmart   http://www.coursesmart.com/
- Flat World Knowledge   http://www.flatworldknowledge.com/
- Kno   http://www.kno.com/features
- Vook   http://vook.com/

E-READERS DEVICES:
- Kindle   https://kindle.amazon.com/
- Nook   http://www.barnesandnoble.com
- Kobo   http://www.kobobooks.com/ereaders
- Reader   http://ebookstore.sony.com/reader/

MEDIA PLATFORMS:
- OverDrive   http://www.overdrive.com/resources/mediaformats/eBooks.aspx
- Axis360   http://www.btol.com/axis360.cfm
- Freading   http://freading.com/index
- EBSCOhost   http://www.ebscohost.com/ebooks
- Ebrary   http://www.ebrary.com
- MyiLibrary   http://lib.myilibrary.com

The expansion of e-collections is tied to innovations in technology which promotes access to digital formats of books, magazines and the like in areas of fiction and non-fiction. Even though budgets are shrinking, patrons' needs and wants are spreading over a wide range of materials formats. Extra-Help Librarians should update themselves on a library's current e-collection goals and acquisitions to provide patrons with sound information regarding digital services. Knowledge about access points, basic troubleshooting, online support links and instructional hand-outs are also necessary.

Databases

Collection development tends to spread a materials' budget over various formats. A large amount of the budget is no longer reserved to books in print because of new digital formats being introduced in the market. Titles often are made available as a book, sound recording and e-book. In addition, databases take a big percentage of the materials' budget. Database usage correlates to staff training and patrons' awareness. Extra-Help Librarians have opportunities to participate in online resources promotions whenever they interact with patrons face-to-face at the reference desk or teach courses.

A wide variety of databases are available to fulfill patrons' information needs. Many of them are replacing books, journals, encyclopedias and other materials. Libraries subscribe to those of interest and relevance to their community. Also, scope, price and usability are taken in consideration. A library's type, size and budget are factored into the number of databases to which it subscribes. There is a great number of general and field specific databases and libraries might include a variety of them in their package. Academic libraries in particular acquire such packages. They are known as "Big Deals" and are used to determine database subscription prices (Kumar, 2011). Quantity, not content, is often a major factor in their acquisitions. "A la Carte" acquisition provides more flexibility and an opportunity to tailor to the library's needs. But it is expensive to select individual choices and many institutions can not afford such an option. Vendors often overlap database content in their packages and it is a challenge to search across different interfaces and platforms. However it has been improving with Federated Searching, which contributes to the increase of database use.

Databases are costly and it is necessary to promote them to patrons as often as possible, guiding and demonstrating how to use them to make these valuable resources known and used more frequently. Patrons need to learn about database's availability, accessibility, content value and their many features to be able to obtain the information they need. Reference and Instruction librarians spend great portion of their time training students on the various databases available. In collaboration with faculty, they decide how to make such resources easily accessible through subject guides and embedding them in courses pages. Public libraries offer workshops on online resources, also including databases. In public and school libraries, it is especially important to show them to parents helping their children with school projects. Even when they ask for print materials, there is usually a chance to introduce the library website and its resources and to emphasize databases. Showing basic features such as full text, citation only—or a combination of both—helps them understand databases better. Such steps prepare parents and children to use databases more frequently and productively.

WEEDING

The collections' weeding goal is to keep useful materials with accurate and current information to efficiently serve patrons needs. Most common problems with books are water damage, broken spines, dirt, stains, scribbles and notes, and currency. Audiovisuals and sound recording materials deteriorate over time, since after so much use they get scratched and cracked, and parts are frequently lost. Extra-Help Librarians handle many of these materials, often processing discards. Policies purpose, how to do something and disposal of weeded items are often well-defined and cover many aspects which are supplemented with staff's directives.

Due to the transient nature of Extra-Help Librarians assignments, follow up measures are important to everyone involved in a project. Weeding in particular has many steps and a progress log or a simple note about the status means a lot to others. Also, even though the weeding guidelines and procedures have standards, they can differ from one location to another. Double-check variations to avoid mistakes. Also, when discarding, verify a material's final destination. Examples are the library's storage for future sales, recycling or other alternatives. Such cautions are due to the fact that Extra-Help Librarians handle projects at various stages and most often over short periods of time. It is always a good idea to double check the assessment criteria for each project too. Weeding assessment considers duplicates, poor condition, outdated and low circulation, for instance.

Disposal of weeded materials can involve donation to other organizations such as Reading Tree (http://www.surplusbooksforcharity.org/), sales through Friends book sales and on Amazon (www.amazon.com) and Craigslist (www.craigslist.com) or other online sales sites, recycling and dumpster options. Ohio Private Academic Libraries—OPAL's weeding guidelines, found at http://staff.opal-libraries.org/resources/user_services/weedingguidelines.pdf, set specific actions in disposing various types of materials.

COMMUNICATION

Connection between libraries and patrons has expanded considerably in the last few decades with the development of the World Wide Web. In addition to in-person and over the telephone interaction, e-mail, online chat and instant message have increased demands on librarians' responsibilities, time and training. Extra-Help Librarians on longer assignments are more likely to be involved in communicating with patrons using these new technologies. Short assignments often do not provide adequate time for support in this area and the lack of continual training also can make it harder to assume these responsibilities when needed.

Delegation of responsibilities to Extra-Help Librarians varies constantly, depending on library location, supervisor, priorities and trust on the professional's abilities. The longer the employment duration, connection with staff, needs of the library and patrons and individual interest and commitment in the library, the more responsibilities are given. Simpler duties might evolve into more complex ones as these factors mix in over time.

EVALUATION CRITERIA OF ONLINE SOURCES

In an increasingly diversified communication environment patrons need to understand how to identify reliable and useful online information. Consequently, evaluation criteria of online sources are necessary. Academic librarians are strongly committed to teach students to be more discerning when doing research on the World Wide Web and to guide them in the use of academic resources. School libraries introduce students to research basics, stressing information evaluation. At public libraries, librarians frequently help patrons to connect or navigate through websites and provide guidance on online searches.

Patrons in general and students in particular, need to develop critical thinking skills when searching online source, free or fee based. Extra-Help Librarians are also responsible for presenting the pitfalls of online research to patrons at public, academic and school libraries. Concerns about the subject matter, information channel, intent behind the content, how it is conveyed and who authored it are some of the aspects which need to be considered. Evaluation of online sources generally includes these points:

- Accuracy
- Audience
- Bias
- Consistency
- Copyright
- Currency
- Format
- Navigation
- Purpose
- Reliability
- Appropriateness
- Authority
- Completeness
- Content
- Credibility
- Depth
- Link
- Objectivity
- Relevancy
- Scope

Many valuable websites are accessible to provide trustworthy information, but patrons often experience the frustrations of doing online searches. They may retrieve unrelated results from a variety of sites or sources and may not have the skills to weed through them to obtain reliable content. In public libraries, often patrons are not even aware of the basic recognition of URL domains extensions such as .edu, .gov, .com, .pro, .info, .biz, .museum. Therefore, the quality of their search results is questionable. Awareness and usage of evaluation criteria benefit older and younger online resource users. As an example, students are more technology savvy and have had more exposure to resource evaluation during their school years, but they can still produce unsatisfactory research papers. Extra-Help Librarians in schools and academic libraries are more likely to be involved in teaching literacy classes. In public libraries they often provide computer assistance to patrons and encounter opportunities to guide them in improving search results.

WEBSITES

Library websites are major sources of information, allowing access from home, office or any other location. It expands the library's reach to a number of people that would not otherwise use the library. Consequently, it impacts library services, librarians work and patrons library usage. In public libraries, more traditional services such as programming for storytime and book discussion, continue to be an in-house staple. Exceptions may exist when story time takes place in childcare facilities and book discussions are held in elderly communities, as part of outreach. Other services have been modified or created due to the new digital environment. This is the case with catalogs, which are now available online. Databases and blogs have been added. Librarians are innovating and acquiring new skills to perform in this new environment. Patrons have more flexible options on how they use libraries to obtain what they need. Instead of walking in the building to get materials, or making requests over the phone, the library website is the portal. It can facilitate transactions for regular patrons and even attract those that might not use the library otherwise.

Each library has its own brand, image or personality and it can be publicized through its website. The interface is uniform to everyone, benefiting employees and patrons. This common tool is a great asset to Extra-Help Librarians because it is consistent and under continuing maintenance. Library systems with several libraries add specific webpages pertaining to its branches or campus location, featuring local programs and news. Extra-Help Librarians quickly locate information when they keep up with changes. Learning to use the general website and local webpages they can guide patrons step by step through the search process.

Libraries websites contain some standard features and links (Dempsey, 2009) even though sometimes they are under different names or designations. They differ first of all in their interface design, but show many similarities in the structure of the information presented. The list below contains common features found in most of them.

- About the Library
- Articles and Databases
- Ask a Librarian
- A-Z Index
- Blogs
- Calendar of Events
- Catalog Search Box
- Contact Us
- Databases
- Disclaimer
- Employment/Human Resources
- FAQ
- Help

- Interlibrary Loan
- Last Updated
- Library Branches/ Campus
- Library Cards Information
- Library Hours
- Make a Donation
- Maps (campus, branches)
- My Account
- News
- Services
- Social Networks Links
- Site Search Box

Other features are specific to academic and public libraries and to schools' media centers. For instance, citation style is found in academic and school libraries' websites. Public and school libraries usually link to award-winning reading lists. In regards to usage, an academic library's website data can demonstrate that the most used web pages are the library home page, databases, research and how-to guides and pages with general library information (Primary Research Group, 2007). Therefore, website designers continue to modify libraries' websites to improve navigation issues and make content easily accessible.

WEB 2.0 TOOLS

The presence of libraries in various social networks and the development of blogs, wikis, Flickr, and Twitter are examples of common strategies in use to reach more patrons in the online environment. Increase in technology usage has motivated libraries to innovate their outreach programs. Even though Web 2.0 Tools have launched new challenges motivated staff create and maintain library spaces through websites and other communication channels. Each environment attracts different groups of people, requiring unique approaches based on patrons' characteristics and preferences. Using blogs and Twitter to communicate the latest library news and information teasers, libraries can reach a number of patrons that are not necessarily frequent library users.

Building relationship in social networks, libraries share with "fans" common interests, welcomes interactions, and promote services. Online interactions between the library and patrons are not as quantitative as expected compared with other interactive sites that compete with libraries. That is perhaps due to the fact that libraries are supported by local communities differing from competing sites that pull their contributors from the whole country and even the world (Coffman, 2012). A more qualitative examination emphasizes selective social media that works best for the community to create connections (Solomon, 2011), which is ultimately more beneficial for patrons and the library. Widely used social networks with libraries' presence include:

- Facebook   http://facebook.com
- LinkedIn   http://linkedin.com
- Second Life   http://secondlife.com
- Twitter   https://twitter.com

Libraries are present in online communities, but the initiative requires continuing maintenance and the monitoring of contacts, comments and addition of content. Clear goals and guidelines on staff duties and responsibilities facilitate the upkeep of the library postings. Custom social network platforms are available, but the levels of funds and staff commitment are substantial obstacles that can delay libraries' engagement.

Personal interest and know-how enter into account as librarians engage in Web 2.0 initiatives. Also, procedures and guidelines on library presence in social networks help librarians' involvement in terms of contributions from their area, time allocation and training. Many libraries have created specific social network policies, in particular for Facebook. Examples include the Holmes County District Public Library (http://www.holmeslibrary.org/aboutus/facebook-policy/) and Morton Grove Public Library (http://www.webrary.org/inside/polfacebook.html). Others, such as Messenger Public Library of North Aurora (http://www.northaurora.lib.il.us/social-media--policy) and University of Louisville (http://louisville.edu/ocm/policies/socialmedia) incorporate several social media in one policy.

Another type of promotion tool frequently used by libraries is YouTube (http://www.youtube.com). There is vast amount of library related information available in this online communication vehicle. For instance, videos on library events and instructional lessons are produced to market the library presence online, as well as to disseminate information outside of the library walls, making information accessible to students and to share content with other institutions. Also, the library contributes to non-traditional patrons who otherwise might not learn about the resources the library possesses.

Library use of communication tools to expand its presence—especially in the online world—demands time, efforts and financial investments. Many initiatives might not meet quantifiable expectations. However, they represent libraries' continuing interest in diversifying their outreach and in staying current. In such context, Extra-Help Librarians need to be knowledgeable about the libraries' active presence in the online world to support staff in any way needed. Knowledge of the process and importance of reviews, rankings and tagging and their awareness of sites such as Twitter, Facebook and others can be valuable for those librarians interested in permanent positions in other categories.

VIRTUAL REFERENCE

The increase in technology tools and their usage by patrons has prompted libraries to incorporate a variety of options to respond to reference questions and facilitate access to information. Adoption of e-mails, instant messaging or other live conference capabilities into reference expanded the way patrons and librarians interact. Evolving from face-to-face, telephone, and snail mail reference to the incorporation of email, chats, and live reference, has brought virtual reference to improved level of service. Each has its advantages. In e-mail services, for instance, the response time can be pre-set up to 24 hours, or as desired, and they are usually handled by in-house librarians. The 24/7 service is more complex, dependent on staff time and scheduling, especially when libraries join a consortium to provide the service. Real-time reference should take in consideration the community, library staff and budget. Examples of services include:

- 24/7 Reference
- DesktopStreaming
- AOL Instant Messenger
- DigiChat

- Groopz
- HumanClick
- LiveAssistance
- NetMeetin
- WebLine
- GroupBoards
- LivePerson
- Livehelper
- QuestionPoint

Virtual reference has become a common and often an expected library service. There are many arrangements. Some libraries manage their own systems; others join in groups and share responsibilities. Below are examples of public libraries' real-time reference services:

InfoLive!	Houston Public Library
Ask-a-Librarian	Live University of Pittsburg
InfoLine	Queens Borough Pub Lib
QandANJ.org	New Jersey Library Network

Delegation of virtual reference responsibilities to Extra-Help Librarians occurs mostly when they are engaged in long assignments or when they have experience with the system, increasing the chances of same day assignments involving this task. Many fee based, open source, and inexpensive software are available to support virtual reference. A few examples are listed below:

- Libraryh3lp — http://libraryh3lp.com/
- LiveZilla — http://www.livezilla.net/home/en/
- Pidgin — http://www.pidgin.im/
- Trillian — http://www.trillian.im/

Easy access to information from anywhere, and in many cases at any time, is a considerable advantage but an evaluation of services states that it has not fulfilled its expectations (Coffman, 2012). There is also concern about its quality. Badly executed sessions include underutilized reference interviews, quality of sources, length of sessions, and unsatisfactory customer service (Zino, 2009). These conclusions affect Extra-Help Librarians involved in virtual reference and they should be aware of these issues.

GAMING

People have played games for thousands of years, serving as a means of entertainment, interactions amongst strangers, family and friends and as a learning tool. There are many types of games which evolved from unstructured games to board games, and more recently, to video and online games. The development of the personal computer has introduced innumerous games to the market and their extensive use has generated psychological and physical concerns to some. For instance, children's gaming has the potential to lead to game addiction, violence, solitary confinement and sedentary habits. Online gaming popularity has added other fears such as over-stimulation, exposure to bad language, spreading of prejudices and harassment. On the other hand, game playing provides opportunities to form groups and even new friendships. Contacts start first around specific game interest and can turn into comments and discussion of other subjects. Gaming can also develop community, reach new audiences and increase library relevance especially to parents and teens (Neiburger, 2007).

Gaming Day @ your library is celebrated in November, but all year long libraries can be engaging their patrons using a variety of games. Public and school libraries are in the forefront of game acquisition and patrons' usage is reported on http://librarygamingtoolkit.org/history.html and http://librarygamelab.org/gamesschoolwork.pdf. As in school libraries, academic libraries' games are used to support educational goals in areas such as information literacy (http://library.uncg.edu/game/). Over the years libraries have used treasure hunt games and board games to disseminate information and involve the community in fun activities. More recently they have been offering video games for checkout and have also scheduled programs using computer video games to bring young patrons together. Libraries such as Ann Harbor Public Library, Bloomington Public Library and many others (http://www.libsuccess.org/index.php?title=Libraries_Hosting_Gaming_Programs) are developing game collections and sponsoring gaming events based on patrons interests and participation. The investments required to develop and maintain the video game collection, promote events and other related issues worth exploring are:

- Staffing
- Programming format (open play versus tournaments)
- Ownership and demand
- Circulation procedures, damage fees, etc.
- Game content and formats
- Equipment (hardware and software)
- Online security (dedicated computers, virus protection and filters)
- Internet connection upgrades (public computers and WiFi)
- Goals: promote reading (stories, roles, reviews cheat sheet,) research (history, sports), writing (about games or creation of stories or worlds) drawing (concepts and design), and careers (new opportunities—fun and profitable jobs)
- ESRB video game rating system

Extra-Help Librarians support patrons of all ages, overseeing children's gaming on public computers, informing young adults about specialized gaming blogs and magazines or exchanging ideas with parents about gaming, behaviors and other developments. In addition, there are opportunities to help during treasure hunts. These require collection knowledge, organization of materials, and supervision of students, parents and teachers involved. Game nights can also require Extra-Help Librarians to help with preparation for the event, as well as players' guidance and supervision. It is also necessary to stay up-to-date on gaming policies, programming and collection.

POTENTIAL PROBLEMS

Staff training on customer service skills, standards of behavior policies and security measures are some of the strategies developed to curb conflicts at libraries. Extra-Help Librarian's familiarity with a library and correlated departments make it easier to orient patrons, forward suggestions. Each library has its own set of problems, but most issues listed below are shared by many libraries:

PEOPLE
- Anger
- Loitering
- Complaints (staff, collection gaps, catalog, related to other patrons, etc)
- Adult disturbance (loudness)
- Children running
- Students behavior

TECHNICAL
- Software questions (Word, PowerPoint)
- Difficulty accessing the internet and Wi-Fi
- Reservation system (computers, requests on print, e-books, courses materials)
- Download issues (process, time, materials availability)
- Account access or status
- Password/PIN number
- Copyright (magazines/journal articles, book content, images download)
- Confidentiality concerns (patrons personal record, staff information)
- Copier and printer machines (work failure, money refund)
- Holds notification failure (mail, phone, e-mail)s
- E-reserves

CIRCULATION
- Overdue fees negotiation (guide to manager/librarian in charge)
- Materials delivery delays
- Claims return of materials (missing, lost)

MISCELLANEOUS
- Study rooms or community room reservation
- Acquisition suggestions
- Emergencies (patron's health threats, facilities leaks and clogs, natural disasters, etc.)

Extra-Help Librarians' preparedness to solve problems—ranging from technology frustrations to medical emergencies while working under supervision or solo—need to be addressed. Outcomes depend in part on their ability to seek directives and follow procedures. Training on a variety of issues and possible scenarios are advised.

SECURITY & SAFETY

University and college campuses and large urban libraries usually have a special unit or security guards in charge to check on patron's behavior and to provide protection whenever necessary. Otherwise, the librarian in charge or the designated staff member is responsible for patrons and staff safety. Extra-Help Librarians need to know how to handle unexpected situations, follow procedures accordingly and write incidents and accidents reports whenever necessary. Some occurrences are related to:

- Collection damage, loss, theft and circulation fees
- Staff and patrons risk, injury, and inappropriate behavior
- Opening (activate and neutralize security gates, alarm)
- Closure (announcements, check various areas of public and staff use, activate alarm)
- Check fire, smoke, heat and gas detectors
- Lighting, ramps, elevators and parking lot safety
- Know security guard rounds schedule and direct line contact
- Evacuation drills (fire, threats, earthquake, tornadoes, flood, etc)
- Emergency supplies location (first aid kit, water, flashlight, etc)
- Location or how to shut off water, gas, and heat equipments

It may sound overwhelming and it can be disastrous when the need arises and there is a lack of knowledge about it. Extra-Help Librarians on daily assignments and covering various locations really need to remember some of the most basic responses to security and safety. A simple example is to know the location of emergency exits doors. Emergency response procedures can be accessible in succinct forms, specifying and listing the potential risk, planned action and response, person in charge and emergency contact number (Kahn, 2008).

INCIDENT REPORT

A problem's seriousness and frequency might require documentation in the form of an incident report. The manager, supervisor or librarian in charge might be responsible for writing about the incident. In case the Extra-Help Librarian is working solo, or in charge, she/he should take the necessary steps. Know where the forms are located in print or available via intranet. Approach a problem critically. Report the facts accurately and objectively. Also, be concise but include enough details in case witnesses are not available and if subsequent actions are needed. Administration awareness of the need to train Extra-Help Librarians on this subject, give them guidance on how to proceed in facing problematic situations and how to produce accurate reports afterwards can benefit all parties involved.

STAFF RELATIONS

Managers and supervisors motivate, delegate and keep workers up-to-date about any changes in the workplace. Their management style and personalities determine work delegation and even how it is accomplished. Managers' administrative skills are identified through variations on workload, projects planning and delegation and communication clarity. Therefore, Extra-Help Librarians provide the best staff support possible when they understand these factors, as well as managers' priorities and expectations. Getting work accomplished in an efficient and timely manner and developing interpersonal relations with local staff also matters significantly.

Even though Extra-Help Librarians float from place to place, the impression they leave through their work and how they relate to staff is important. Acknowledging co-workers, showing interest in how they do their job and gratitude for their help in accomplishing a task makes for stronger relationships and work collaboration. A gratifying work environment depends a lot on the attitude amongst co-workers. Because Extra-Help Librarians often are not in the same location for long periods of time and are not involved in workplace intrigues and conflicts, there is usually more receptivity to their presence if they make a sincere effort to befriend other employees.

In addition, relating well with people might increase the chances to be welcomed back in any location and even lead to more work. Follow the institution procedures to avoid signs of favoritism which generate co-workers resentment. Positive attitude, work ethics, clear communication with managers, supervisors, fellow librarians, circulation staff and other categories are indispensable for Extra-Help Librarians success in the workplace.

INSTITUTIONAL PARTICIPATION

Meetings and committees are unquestionably important opportunities for librarians to provide input on issues and services that impact their work and patrons. However, Extra-Help Librarians often are not included in work meetings. It is understandable when the agenda is not relevant to them or they are covering for other staff to attend these meetings. But their inclusion in staff meetings offer them opportunities to stay up-to-date with changes, discuss problems and be part of staff dynamics.

Depending on the library size committees are formed to discuss a variety of issues. Their recommendations frequently turn into policies and procedures in areas of collection development, addition of services, patrons' appropriate behavior and in other ways. Extra-Help Librarians could be allowed to participate in applicable groups. Their knowledge of the library structure, personnel and patrons in various locations would add a unique perspective to committees' discussions and potential outcomes.

Libraries that limit such participation lose valuable insights and at the same time reduce Extra-Help Librarians' learning opportunities. Participation can translate into engagement and better staff interpersonal relations. When lacking ways to involve the category at these levels, institutions perhaps could create other avenues for Extra-Help Librarians to express their concerns and suggestions about their work and how they fit in the system. By using meetings, surveys, performance evaluations and other useful mechanisms to receive feedback, libraries could show inclusiveness, ultimately benefiting themselves, the employees and patrons.

PROFESSIONAL ASSOCIATIONS

Membership to librarians' associations at local, state and national levels offers opportunities to be up-to-date in current professional issues, exchange ideas through networking, collaborate with other groups and volunteer. They represent full-time and part-time workers, including in the latter category the interests of Extra-Help Librarians. Even though this category concerns are not top priority in discussions, they indirectly benefit from advocacy efforts. Perhaps associations should take the initiative to form a group/committee to discuss Extra-Help Librarians topics of interest. However, it should be considered that the category's innate uncertainties serve as deterrent to joining professional associations. Also, participation in association meetings and conferences can be difficult because of their limited income and the lack of libraries' financial support for such enterprises.

Each library association produces its own magazine and maintains a website with an extraordinary wealth of information. A list of some professional library associations, example of their publications and website address is shown here for further exploration.

Association	Publication	Website
ALA—American Library Association	American Libraries Magazine	http://americanlibrariesmagazine.org/
PLA—Public Library Association	Public Libraries Magazine	http://www.ala.org/pla/publications/publiclibraries
ACRL—Association of College and Research Libraries	College and Research Libraries News	http://crln.acrl.org/
AASL—American Association of School Libraries	Knowledge Quest	http://www.ala.org/aasl/knowledgequest

Table No. 2.2. Librarians' Associations

Library issues and events are covered by several journals, magazines, news media outlets, blogs and other entities. Extra-Help Librarians may take advantages of these resources to develop their skills, especially if they aspire to be employed in other librarian categories. There are a variety of magazines and journals with focus on librarianship in general and specific subject areas. Some of them are:

- Journal of Academic Librarianship
- Library Journal
- School Library Journal
- Reference and User Services Quarterly
- Community and Junior College Libraries
- College and Research Libraries
- Journal of Academic Librarianship
- Reference and User Services Quarterly
- Serials Librarian
- Information Outlook
- Reference Services Review
- Reference Librarian
- Library Trends
- Computer in Libraries
- Information Technologies and Libraries
- Journals of Library Administration

Professional publications are accessible tools in several ways. Join a particular association and their magazine, journal or newsletter comes as part of the benefits. The fact that Extra-Help Librarians income is lower than other categories, inquiry about reduced membership rates. Other ways to read these publications is to through the local library. Individual libraries usually subscribe to some of them, making print and online versions available to staff. Perhaps print copies are kept on limited access with reference materials but patrons just need to ask to be able to read them. Other alternative to access professional publications is through libraries' databases. It is not uncommon either for some publications to post some of their articles online for free.

LISTSERVS

Also known as professional electronic mailing list or email groups, listserv members share valuable information. Subscription to a listserv of interest or a field specialty provides opportunity for exchange of theoretical and practical knowledge. It is another way to stay up-to-date with current issues in libraries. Participants become part of a community, sharing experiences, providing suggestions and supporting each others needs and initiatives. Members' communication is supervised by the list administrator. Using appropriate discussion etiquette, questions are posted and comments are added. There are listservs for innumerable subjects and selection depends on the interest and activity of the group. Listserv lists are available through LisWiki (http://liswiki.org/wiki/Discussion_groups#Directories_of_Library_Discussion_Groups) and Web Guides (http://www.loc.gov/rr/program/bib/libsci/guides.html#listservs). Here are some examples:

LISTSERV	SUBSCRIPTION BY EMAIL	FOCUS
LIBREF-L	listserve@listserv.kent.edu	Reference
PUBLIB	listserv@webjunction.org	Public Libraries
PUBYAC	pubyac-join@lists.lis.illinois.edu	Young Adult and Children
CALIBK12	calibk12@groups.google.com	California Library Media Teachers
INFOLIT	infolit@ala.org	Information literacy (school, academic, and public libraries)
ILI-L	ili-l@ala.org	Information Literacy Instruction

Table No. 2.3. Listservs by Area of Interest

Reference & Patron Assistance

All kinds of questions are handled at the reference or information desk. There are challenging queries that require more in-depth investigation, use of complex search strategies and resources, but directional and technical questions are common. Librarians make efforts to provide patrons with what they need, using print and online collections at hand or obtaining materials through interlibrary loans when necessary. Factors such as patrons' research deadlines and materials format requirements or preferences, as well as resource access and availability come into consideration. In addition, reference materials in print are decreasing due to infrequent use, reduced budgets and easy access to online information (Danford, 2010).

Extra-Help Librarians often have limited exposure to local print collections, so when there is a need to search sources that provide fast returns, online reference resources may be useful. Governmental and professional associations, commercial organizations and other online sources are used to retrieve results beyond the collection owned. The World Catalog site supplements the library catalog searches for books, articles and sound recording. Even Amazon.com can be used to identifying books, series, and more.

Extra-Help Librarians learn the collection and the tools used to search for responses timely and accurately. Updates on current changes in a library or system make it easier for them to handle patron's information needs at the reference desk. Frequent training also maximizes outcomes, particularly in the following areas.

LIBRARY CATALOG

This is one of the most important tools that enable librarians and patrons to find library materials. The evolution from paper based catalogs to the present computerized systems radically changed the way materials are located. Stored records have a combination of assigned fields for title, author, subject, Dewey number, ISBN number, barcode and other areas. The option of using basic or advanced searches is a major advantage of online catalog. Learning how to use it thoroughly helps librarians perform efficiently and quickly.

Extra-Help Librarians experience with library catalogs facilitates the instruction of patrons on how to search the collection. Before being librarians they were patrons themselves and familiar with libraries' catalogs. However, most of the time librarians use specialized catalog systems to search library collections. Besides being different from the library's web based catalog that patrons often use, specialized systems provide more powerful search features. They can connect the catalog with circulation, allow access to statistics and patrons records and other technology devices.

Catalog systems vary from one library to another and types vary according to the companies that sell and maintain them or provide upgrades and technical support. Training is necessary to learn how to use a system and libraries offer them to employees on their own or through the companies that they are in contract with. There are many types of library automated systems and their evaluation can be explored at http://www.librarytechnology.org/perceptions2012.pl (Breeding, 2013). These are examples of proprietary and open-source systems available in the market:

- Ex Libris Group   http://www.exlibrisgroup.com/category/Voyager
- Destiny   http://www.follettsoftware.com/ezform.cfm?ezid=275&urlRef=movetodestiny
- Horizon, Symphony, Unicorn   http://www.sirsidynix.com
- LibraryWorld   http://www.libraryworld.com
- Millennium   http//www.iii.com/products/millennium_ils.shtml
- Voyager   http://www.exlibrisgroup.com/category/Voyager
- Atriuum   http://www.booksys.com/v2/products/
- Alexandria   http://www.companioncorp.com/mediawiki/index.php/Alexandria
- Evergreen   http://evergreen-ils.org/
- CDS Invenio   http://invenio-software.org/#
- Koha   http://koha-community.org/
- NewGenLib   http://www.verussolutions.biz/web/
- OpenBiblio   http://obiblio.sourceforge.net/

CATALOG ASSISTANCE

Patrons often have questions about the catalog and it is one of a librarian's responsibilities to teach them how to use it efficiently. Depending on how comfortable patrons are with computers in public libraries they present some behavior patterns. There are those that refuse to learn to use a computer and there are older patrons that even miss card catalogs. Others are not familiar with the library catalog or are not able to find the item for which they are looking. Another group might just not be clear about which computers are available for catalog searches—even if the hardware has a sign on it. Also, some patrons just prefer human interaction through face-to-face contact rather than search the catalog themselves. Consequently, they come to librarians to help them with their search needs. The approach is to reassure patrons that they will be helped and, whenever possible, give clear explanations on how to use the catalog. That might even motivate them to search materials on their own.

Public, school and academic library patrons have different levels of difficulty using the catalog. Some of them regularly offer catalog instructions classes to remedy common problems. Of course, catalog know-how is just one of the steps of patron's research process. In general, school and academic libraries are more heavily oriented on instruction in part due to the complexity of their clientele's subject-based assignments.

TECHNOLOGY & EQUIPMENT ASSISTANCE

Technology development is quickly making other equipments obsolete. Patrons' use of typewriters, pay phones, microfiche and microfilm readers, tape and CD players, overhead/transparency projectors and TV sets are being replaced by others apparatus. The transition to new equipment and operations requires professional support from the library staff. Extra-Help Librarians often demonstrate to patrons how to use equipment and they pass suggestions or complaints to other staff. Therefore, it is necessary to know how to troubleshoot equipment problems and report them to appropriate personnel.

Clearly, ownership of typewriters has been reduced to very few places such as small libraries or regional branches. These machines are legacies of the past, but there are still patrons that inquire about their availability. Paper forms are still being filled out using a typewriter, so they are not completely out of use. Microfilm and microfiche reader are other machine types that continue to be used and patrons need assistance on how to use them to do their research.

On a more current note, increases in cell phone ownership have drastically cut, or even eliminated, payphones or access to telephones owned by libraries. Extra-Help Librarians need to know each library guideline on public usage of the reference telephone (usually permitted on a case by case basis), the rules on cell phone use and on live computer chats or conference calls (laptop users can make personal and business connections). Complaints can be handled professionally by presenting the library's rules on appropriate behavior to the patron.

The type and size of a library can influence how computers are set up for patrons to use. Large public libraries might opt for the separation of computers by task, designating some for catalog searches, general online access and word processing. Allocating space for catalogs near entrances or around reference areas and online access computers in a particular area diminish patrons' confusion. School and academic libraries tend to have combined computer tasks on the same terminal in designated areas, sometimes called a Media Center or a Student Commons.

Copier or print stations require close supervision. Patrons often disregard operating instructions. Coin, paper money or pay-card problems often require intervention. Machine breakdowns are not uncommon. Keep handy the contact number for the technician or the servicing company's customer service number. Once again, troubleshooting skills are necessary to handle dissatisfied patrons and machine problems.

Assistance might be needed too to set up laptops, TV or a projector for a lecture in the classroom, media center or any event at the community room. At times we forget the fact that libraries are at different stages in adopting technology tools, especially when students can borrow laptops and e-readers devices at some academic and school libraries. Availability and rules on the use of these items are institution specific. Be prepared, but Extra-Help Librarians in such environments might neither work directly nor have control over the delivery of these equipments. This can be particularly true when other staff members, such as student aids, clerks, technicians or others, are in charge of them.

Patrons in general might request information about software requirements, networking capabilities, access, website security or other matters. It is important to find out the answers or guide them to resources which provide useful explanations. In-house Information Technology department might be easy to reach when more complex technical support is needed. When providing services such as book downloads and e-books, tutorials or quick guides can answer basic questions, but more complex problems might be handled by vendors.

Overall, guidance is often necessary and Extra-Help Librarians can be exposed to unpredictable equipment problems and patrons' frustrations in such contexts. Interpersonal skills are essential to work through the mechanics of the problem and the emotional charges that can emanate from situations of this nature.

RESERVATIONS

Reservation of library space and computers are tasks that Extra-Help Librarians may be expected to handle, interacting with patrons to explain, supervise or train. Each one has their own set of steps that need to be learned, so the professional is able to provide correct information and better serve the users, whether they are individuals or organizations.

Once a library leaves behind patrons' paper sign-up for computers, and gets automated software to manage the flow of computer users, librarians are assigned to supervise the service unless library technicians are assigned such task. Extra-Help Librarians also incorporate this function. Patrons need to be trained on how to use the system. Especially in public libraries where there is a constant flow of new users, there is always a need to guide them through the computer reservations steps. An advantage is that the reservations and print capabilities are integrated. Reservation systems (Enis, 2012) differ and some of the ones available are:

- Userful Pre-Book   http://www2.userful.com/products/userful-pre-book
- PC Reservation   http://www.envisionware.com/pcres
- Pharos System   http://www.pharos.com/signUp/pharos-signup-LIB.html
- Cassie   http://www.librarica.com/
- LTP: One   http://www.envisionware.com/lptone/
- Re'Quest & PrintQuest   http://www.iteamaccess.com/products1.htm
- SAM   http://www.comprisetechnologies.com/?page_id=28

Community rooms, exhibit halls, meeting rooms and auditoriums are additional library spaces usually open for use by other organizations, for free or for a fee. Regulations regarding reservations and usage are some of the aspects treated in the libraries' guidelines. Extra-Help Librarians might not handle space reservations because they might not be familiar with space allocation for library programming and events. To avoid reservations conflicts, this responsibility can be assigned to librarians in charge or to managers. However, it is helpful to know the room capacity, the type of organizations that are allowed to reserve the space, the location of reservation request forms and who is responsible for handling reservations. This way they are able to inform and pre-screen applicants, simplifying the process for those that make space reservations.

Library spaces can also be a source of revenues to subsidize other library services. Extra-Help Librarians serving more than one library can improve their comfort level on dealing with inquiries of prospective speakers (Shon, 2006) and of organizations seeking to use library space.

CIRCULATION

Reference and circulation desks share knowledge of patron information at some levels. It is appropriate and sometimes even necessary for Extra-Help Librarians in the academic, school and public areas to learn at least some of the basics. Situations that might require circulation knowledge arise when helping patrons request materials, identifying cause of problems when patrons are not able to access databases with their card number, supporting or supervising circulation desk and in other ways. When working solo or with circulation technicians such information contributes to smoother connection with co-workers and patrons, eliminating problems and providing better service.

The size of a library, whether it is the main or a branch, requires Extra-Help Librarians to be adaptable to staffs' needs. Occasionally, besides working at the reference or information desk, they might be assigned to perform circulation duties. It is an opportunity to expand the understanding of library work, physically handle materials going out and coming in, interact with another layer of personnel and learn more about what they do. Also express appreciation for the circulation staff efforts and demonstrate a team player attitude. Perhaps there will be a chance to meet new patrons and other more independent users who do not necessarily seek librarians' assistance. Considering the responsibilities of each desk, be willing to learn, help, and stay away from interfering more than desired.

During economic hardship budgets are cut and staff reduction becomes a common occurrence. Circulation desk need for librarians help may be an indication of the library's budget impact on personnel. Also, workers' absences and a library's holiday closures, for instance, generate accumulation of work at the circulation desk and more help might be necessary to get the work done quickly to avoid a major back-up of materials. In many circumstances an

Extra-Help Librarians' general knowledge of the circulation staffs' tasks can make considerable difference. Other helpful information includes:

CIRCULATION GLOSSARY BASICS
- Check in, check out
- Claims returned
- Blocks, fees, and payment methods
- Daily reports (cancellation and receipts)
- New library card forms and issuance procedures
- Radio frequency identification (RFID)

CIRCULATION POLICY, PROCEDURES AND GUIDELINES
- Patron categories (resident, visitors, out-of-state, teachers, staff)
- Library card privileges
- Card replacement (free or charges)
- Loan period (owned items, ILL, renewals)
- Fines (cash, checks, credit card payment)
- Damaged or Lost items
- Processing of materials requested by patrons from other libraries

CONFLICT RESOLUTION
- Know the library and patrons rights and responsibilities
- Listen carefully
- Be calm and respectful
- Suggest solutions
- Refer case to supervisor if necessary

Reference & Circulation Statistics

Quantitative and qualitative data are measurement tools that have become increasingly more necessary for libraries. In times of decreasing revenues, the frequent collection of data is even more vital and proves libraries needs. It ultimately influences fund allocation and justifies expenditures or cuts. Library operation hours, personnel use and materials reductions are often based on such accumulative snapshots of the library. Also, data is useful to evaluate collections and services, to track students' progress and to evaluate programming participation. Other activities that libraries sponsor are also affected. Grants, government funding and partnership with other organizations are also influenced by data collection results.

The process used to get the information range from investigative, in-house questionnaires to more elaborate outsourced research. This can depend on the urgency of results and funds available. Data generated automatically or manually (MacDonell, 2007) comes from various sources. Data collection of library usage is obtained through reference, circulation and other services. Online sources—such as digital reference usage, website counters, databases and catalogs, materials acquisition, electronic security systems, circulation transactions—are available automatically. Manual sources involve logs of materials usage at the library. That can include books, magazines, newspapers (utilized, but not checked out), collaborative lessons, patrons printing and photocopying and other sources.

Repeated data collection might be performed at various department levels to obtain an overview of the library. For instance, the frequency and difficulty level of reference questions and computer assistance are aspects revisited in library statistics. Extra-Help Librarians handle statistical data when weeding material, collecting manual data about reference usage and other assigned tasks. Both reference and circulation statistics can involve Extra-Help Librarians. Research frequency and location, as well as their assignment lengths, can affect involvement. Therefore, participation might be for a day or for a longer period of time, in one place or several places. Or Extra-Help Librarians can miss out on participation entirely. Also, it is worth noting that they not just collect data, but also generate it, when providing services.

DIVERSITY

Representing patrons' best interests, libraries play an indispensable role. They identify their community needs and plan strategically to provide services, collections, community outreach and alliances with other organizations to respond adequately. Libraries are gathering centers for all people, regardless of their status, and it plays a primary role in making people feel respected and welcome. Public libraries are widely diverse, bringing together people with different characteristics such as race, religious beliefs and age groups. They also include people who feel disenfranchised, immigrants and minorities. Academic libraries demonstrate strong awareness of diversity issues through campus events, lectures, workshops and entertainment centered on diversity. It provides the academic community opportunities to discuss the matters involved, contributing to a more understanding society. School libraries face similar attentiveness to diversity, reaching out to English as Second Language learners and their parents, who often did not grow up going through the same educational system.

Considering librarians' impact in diverse communities, institutions such as academic libraries require the enclosure of a diversity statement as part of employment applications. Others add interview questions related to the subject. This shows how diversity issues are important in the library system. Professionals such as Extra-Help Librarians, especially those working in various locations, have opportunities to interact with communities, expanding their appreciation for differences. Their respect for all patrons adds to the support of their institution's principles on diversity.

DISABLED PERSONS

Libraries are continually updating their buildings and equipments to better serve patrons and to comply with the American Disability Act (ADA) laws. In the process, materials such as large print books, audiobooks, designated computer stations and shelf aids are acquired to assist disabled persons in utilizing the library. The type and degree of patrons' physical or mental condition—or a combination of both disabilities—affects the level of service (Roberts, 2010). An Extra-Help Librarian's knowledge of how to serve disabled patrons is useful in interacting with them, provide higher quality service and also in granting appropriate application of the library guidelines on disability matters.

Often the location of the library influences the need for adjustment to ADA requirements and services availability. Libraries in major urban areas are more likely to have more pressing needs to comply with the law to accommodate their patrons and there is possibly more advocacy and funds to accomplish the necessary modifications in buildings and services. Less wealthy and remote areas face more difficulties to implement the upgrades. Services also differ by area in regards to a library's collections, equipments, staff expertise and referral system.

Students with disabilities have the support of psychologists and even personal aids, depending on the severity of their problems. Librarians in this setting are more familiar with each case. Extra-Help Librarians need to know the services and practices so they can provide services for students with disabilities when they use the library. In university circles, librarians' coordination with the various departments and the faculty can facilitate continuing adjustments to provide improved accommodations to disabled persons. Overall, libraries maintaining departments that serve patrons with vision, auditory and mobility difficulties—as well as their caregivers and/or relatives—will expect Extra-Help Librarians to have more qualifications to be able to handle the work demands.

SENIOR SERVICES

The 2010 US Census reported that there are 40.3 million people over 65 years old and this group will continue to grow. Libraries planning to involve them ought to consider their needs and expectations. The needs of older patrons vary, but generally they seek a welcoming and safe place, engaging activities and opportunities to learn. Adding to the current senior demographics, baby boomers that are in a transition phase, may serve as mediators for their elderly parents even as they are coming into retirement age themselves (Robins, 2011). Therefore, information needs about health and finances, interest in post-work activities and technology usage tends to keep growing. The trend is also noticeable in technology development where hardware and software are designed or adapted for seniors (McDermott, 2012) and the number of seniors joining social networks (USA Today, 2012).

Libraries are then confronted with opportunities and challenges. ALA's *Keys to Engaging Older Adults @ your library* is one of the initiatives created to involve this growing group. There are even gaming sessions catering to them which aim to benefit them physically and mentally (Danforth, 2010; Roberts, 2011). The effort is not just to serve this group, but also to involve them as contributors to the organization. In all types of libraries volunteering has traditionally been the most common way older patrons make their contribution. Adding to this, they are resourceful speakers, writers, tutors and collaborators, active readers and participants in book discussions.

Interaction with older adults at public libraries takes form in various manners. Those not familiar with new technology often request assistance from librarians to search for information and the catalog. There are those that would rather not use the computers because they lack experience or they might prefer face-to-face contact with staff. Overall, their basic needs include instruction on how to access websites or get their email and referrals to other organizations, such as senior housing providers and free tax preparation help. Libraries' attentiveness to signage, seating, lighting and shelve heights show that they care for these patrons' personal needs.

Academic libraries are serving an increasing number of older adults and seniors going back to colleges to obtain more education for economic and leisure reasons. Colleges and universities offer educational programs that can be attended by those that are still in the workforce, intend to return to the workforce or by those that take online courses for any reason. There are courses also designed to attract educated and financially independent seniors. These lifelong students get enjoyment from what they are leaning and have a desire, not a need, to expand their knowledge. Libraries are challenged to provide more resources at an age of decreasing funding, but they are also devising new strategies to bring this group to the library as patrons and supporters.

Older parents, for natural or adoption reasons, are also found in school libraries, side by side with grandparents. Economic factors also generate more involvement when parents are seeking new employment and have more time to participate in their children's school. Supportive grandparents often are active in their grandchildren's school, since often their children are not able to participate because of work.

Intergenerational programming, exhibits, workshops on culture, history and aging issues—retirement, investing, medical insurance, as examples—are just a few of the topics that are of interest to older adults. Captivating this group of active and education driven patrons through library service adds more diversity to the library mix and is an investment in these potential donors.

Training Extra-Help Librarians on the needs of an older adult generation and of seniors, making resources available and showing them how to serve them appropriately, reflects consistent library goals in providing tailored services to this population group. Understanding social and economic issues are key elements to best respond to their needs and wants.

VOLUNTEERS, FRIENDS OF THE LIBRARY

& LIBRARY FOUNDATION

An understanding of these library supporters depends on a variety of factors such as library needs and organizational structure, as well as each of these supporters' functions and goals. In general, there is not much differentiation of these groups in terms of their goals, since all of them make efforts to support the library. They might work as one entity or separately, but regardless of their bylaws, their contribution to the everyday and long-term functions of libraries is invaluable. They generate support to libraries through donation of time and money and seeking funding through fundraising events and grants, advocating, engaging in community involvement, creating a pool of volunteers and sponsoring services. Most groups work on a volunteer basis, but the more engaged they become in fundraising activities and donor development the need for a paid staff increases.

A library's shortage of funds and staff increases its dependency on volunteers. Smaller libraries often depend on volunteers to stay open. Bigger libraries have designated staff to cover most needs and normally there is a coordinator to assign and supervise volunteers' work. Libraries that are linked to labor unions have very strict limitations on the use of volunteers in the workplace. Therefore, the quantity of volunteers and the extent of work they provide changes according with each library's needs, size and legal structure. Libraries tend to appreciate volunteers support and recognize each individual's contribution.

Extra-Help Librarians have contact with volunteers at various levels, directly or indirectly. That aspect of their work can sometimes overlaps with other aspects, especially in smaller libraries where shelving and mending are not done by library paraprofessionals. There are occasions in which face-to-face contacts occur and other times they just perform interrelated duties. As an example, Extra-Help Librarians weed materials, send them for volunteers to mend, then it goes back to a librarian before shelving. In addition, when Friends maintain a store within the library building, Extra-Help Librarians should know the store hours to inform patrons. Also the type of materials accepted, drop off locations and how to issue tax deductible receipts for donations is useful information.

INTELLECTUAL FREEDOM & CENSORSHIP

The right to read and express ideas is fundamental to society's growth, even if the ideas are unusual or not readily accepted. Libraries support intellectual freedom, and in opposing censorship they have confronted challenges from persons and entities. Public and school libraries are specially targeted. Parents concerned with their children's exposure to sexual content, offensive language and violence, have disputed the access to books and online resources at libraries. However, many ideas and books that were disapproved of once have over the years been accepted. Libraries have implemented initiatives to educate patrons about the need to secure free access to materials. For instance, Banned Books Week (http://www.ala.org/advocacy/banned/bannedbooksweek) promotes awareness, advocating the power of contrasting ideas. School libraries in particular educate students on such matters, developing literary readings, discussions and displays.

Handling of complaints is one example of how Extra-Help Librarians may be involved in the censorship of materials. Regardless of the type of library they work for, they should clearly understand the steps to follow whenever a patron presents a concern or dissatisfaction with collection materials, before any incident arises. What to say to the patron? How about advising the patron to submit a written complaint? Where is the complaint form? Tell the patrons who will receive the form and respond? Any idea how long the process takes? Above all, be an interested listener, reassure the patron that the concerns will be taken in consideration and a response issued.

Additional concerns with privacy and information access have been raised about the usage and ramifications of new technologies. Privately or library-owned devices, such as iPhones, iPads, e-books services, as well as social networks participation, pose restrictions that can infringe individuals rights (Stuart, 2012). Considering the increasing use of technology in libraries, awareness of potential effects on patrons' privacy is necessary to continue to best serve them.

Knowledge of patrons' protection laws at various levels build librarians confidence, enabling them to follow libraries procedures adequately. Examples of documents that play significant roles in intellectual freedom and censorship issues are the Children's Internet Protection Act, U.S. Constitution, USA Patriotic Act, Federal and State Laws on privacy and confidentiality (Chmara, 2009), Library Bill of Rights and the Library's materials selection policies.

COPYRIGHT

Unauthorized use or reproduction of written, images, music and other works is illegal. Patrons' awareness of copyrights and the need to curtail its abuse is fundamental to guarantee that the "fair use" of materials is maintained. Libraries are proactive in securing authors' copyrights. Academic librarians are especially attentive to this matter. They inform students, faculty and staff about collection use and photocopying limitations imposed by copyright laws, post signs by copiers, give workshops, and motivate teachers to review students' assignments to detect plagiarism. Faculty classroom handouts and request for library reserves of copyrighted works is also under limitations. In school libraries efforts are made to introduce students to author contact and works, as well as the importance of bibliographic citation. Public libraries serve a wide range of patrons and the fair use doctrine is a basis for free access to materials that otherwise could not be available to those who do not have the economic means to obtain them on their own. Therefore, in this setting the need for restriction on reproduction of materials is emphasized.

Extra-Help Librarians share the responsibility to assist patrons to become aware of copyright laws as stated by the US Copyrights Office (http://www.copyright.gov/fls/fl102.htm) and ALA (http://www.ala.org/advocacy/copyright/copyrightarticle/whatfairuse). Other resources include libraries which post copyright polices on their websites. For example, the University of California Los Angeles makes available various copyright policies accessible at http://www.library.ucla.edu/copyright/ucla-copyright-policy

MARKETING

Libraries are dedicated to providing valuable service to the community and quality customer service to all users. It makes efforts to maintain loyal users, partners and collaborators. Even though libraries are not especially known for their marketing efforts, they have over the years taken advantage of one of the most common marketing tools in the word-of-mouth strategy. Considering that other information sources are growing and the competition is increasing, the library's marketing strategies should be clearly stated. As other employees, Extra-Help Librarians need to be aware of their institution's marketing approaches to convey the messages to patrons professionally and effectively.

Marketing strategies for libraries involve a combination of various mediums which form the marketing mix. Some of the components are stated below:

- Signage
- Collections (books, digital, local history)
- Testimonials
- Displays
- Newsletter
- Events/Programming

- Co-curricular engagements
- Blogs
- Bulletin board
- University Press publications
- Website
- Podcasts
- Social Network
- Conference presentation

OUTREACH

Internal and external library outreaches are also components of libraries' promotion tools. Programming is a primary vehicle of internal outreach to current and potential patrons. Some examples of this type of outreach are art exhibits, lectures, movie festivals, music and theater performances, book fairs, in-house storytime and book discussions and after school activities. External outreach is a joint enterprise with other organizations such as daycare facilities, hospitals, elderly communities, recycling facilities and student housing for example. Through such initiatives, libraries can showcase their products and services, strengthen partnerships and develop new membership. In phases of financial crisis, outreach tends to shrink, which can diminish community exposure and advocacy involvement.

Usually Extra-Help Librarians are mainly assigned to everyday operations and outreach opportunities are then limited to internal tasks, such as leading library tours for school children or university students, introducing performers when working solo and informing patrons about services and activities. There are few chances to be directly involved with student unions, campus wide events, community schools, senior citizens, homebound patrons, day care centers and others. However, it is important for them to respond appropriately to the marketing strategies in place.

PROMOTIONAL MATERIALS

Vast amounts of promotional materials are produced to inform patrons of continuing services and upcoming activities. Examples of regularly used tools are class catalogs, pamphlets, bookmarks, newsletters, monthly calendars, flyers, lists of new acquisitions and banners and posters. It can be challenging to Extra-Help Librarians to know about every single current and upcoming event, since libraries in different locations frequently plan local events not offered throughout the system or campus.

Promotional materials are issued in print, posted on the library website and delivered to online mediums such as professional associations and listservs, social networks and blogs. Consequently, Extra-Help Librarians have to be attentive to the library promotional efforts. They need to be able to access information quickly and, when necessary, guide patrons to obtain it on their own either at that point or in the future. For example, a libraries' calendar of events is usually available in print and online. It illustrates one marketing item in two different formats and accessible through two or more different channels.

The responsibility to stay up-to-date on a library's events rests not just on supervisors or managers but also on an Extra-Help Librarian's self-motivation to seek ways to stay current. They can navigate the library website and check on banners, programs, lectures or displays or they can hand out print materials and other initiatives to inform patrons appropriately.

LITERARY, PROFESSIONAL & STUDENT AWARDS

There are many national and international awards for specific age groups and book genres and libraries use them in a number of ways. They are utilized to promote writing and motivate readership. Besides reviews, collection development relies on awards to determine purchases. Also, they raise readers' interest on current issues, research and leisure readings. In Academic libraries professional awards focus on research in various fields. Public and school library, in particular, acquire a great number of award winner books to promote reading for skills and leisure.

Extra-Help Librarians can contribute to the dissemination of titles that have been awarded when they make reading recommendations. They can also refer to them for anthologies and citations or as guides for students' research. There are a variety of book awards and the most popular are in literature. There are a few presented below by age group:

CHILDREN
- John Newbery Medal
  http://www.ala.org/alsc/awardsgrants/bookmedia/newberymedal/newberymedal
- Randolph Caldecott Medal
  http://www.ala.org/alsc/awardsgrants/bookmedia/caldecottmedal/caldecottmedal
- The Laura Ingalls Wilder Medal
  http://www.ala.org/alsc/awardsgrants/bookmedia/wildermedal/wilderpast
- The Pura Belpré Award
  http://www.ala.org/alsc/awardsgrants/bookmedia/belpremedal/belprepast
- Coretta Scott King Award
  http://www.ala.org/emiert/cskbookawards/recipients

YOUNG ADULT
- The Michael L. Printz Award
  http://www.ala.org/yalsa/printz
- Young Reader's Choice Award
  http://www.pnla.org/yrca

ADULTS
- National Book Award
  http://www.nationalbook.org/nba2010.html

- Nobel Prize in Literature
  http://www.nobelprize.org/nobel_prizes/literature/laureates/

Also, The New York Times (http://www.nytimes.com/best-sellers-books/overview.html) adult and children's fiction and non-fiction bestsellers lists can guide patrons' reading choices. Extra-Help Librarians should stay abreast of the newest hotlists to inform patrons about the high interest books and the request lists of such items through the library. Many patrons request new books online, others prefer to do it in person at the library.

Academic libraries are impacted to a lesser degree by these awards because of their focus on research and professional pursuits. Therefore, there are other types of awards that are more closely related to these goals. University presses, professional associations and endowments award authors that make significant contribution to the advancement of knowledge. Some examples are listed below:

- The American Book Awards
  http://www.beforecolumbusfoundation.com/aba.html
- Choice Outstanding Academic Book Award
  http://www.cro2.org/default.aspx?page=about_oat&pid=2870805
- National Best Books
  http://bookcritics.org/awards/

The Association of College and Research Libraries (ACRL) provides detailed information about professional awards given to different areas and categories. In its website it divides the awards in the following categories: Achievement and Distinguished Service; Research Awards and Grants and Publications. Also, student awards are made available by institutions, associations, companies by application for recognition of an exceptional writing on issues, travel and participation on professional conferences. This can depend on school enrollment and other eligibility requirements for rewards as indicated below:

- Academic Travel Awards for Students, Post-Doctoral Fellows and Junior Faculty
- Student Awards
- Alan Gent Distinguished Student Paper Award.

Awards and a great number of scholarships need to be promoted to the academic community and librarians offer guidance to many of the resources, procedures and requirements. Therefore, Extra-Help Librarians should be prepared to provide information, make referrals to organizations or to other campus departments better equipped to handle specific matters.

Professional organizations are sources of marketing information, ideas, materials and other items. ACRL (http://www.ala.org/acrl/issues/marketing/), for instance, offers an expanse of options and the American Marketing Association, especially its webcasts (http://www.

marketingpower.com/_layouts/Reference/Webcast.aspx), contains valuable innovative marketing ideas that can be adapted to libraries.

Choose Privacy Week, Summer Reading, School Library Month and Banned Books Week are examples (http://www.ala.org/conferencesevents/celebrationweeks) of libraries' efforts to market library services to users aiming to increase participation and awareness about these and other issues. Extra-Help Librarians take part in the promotion of services and events to patrons. In all types of libraries they have such responsibility.

──────────── CHAPTER REFERENCES ────────────

Breeding, M. (2013). Perceptions 2012: *An international survey of library automation.* Retrieved from http://www.librarytechnology.org/perceptions2012.pl

Brumley, R. (2006). *The reference librarian's policies, forms, guidelines and procedures handbook: with CD-Rom.* New York: Neal-Schuman Publishers.

Chmara, T (2009). *Privacy and confidentiality issues: a guide for libraries and their lawyers.* Chicago, IL: ALA.

Coffman, S. (2012). The decline and fall of the library empire. *Searcher,* 20, 3, Apr.

Danforth, L. (2010). Kleiman on Gaming for Seniors. *Library Journal,* Sep, 135, 15, 44-44.

Danford, N. (2009). The lonely stand of print reference. *Publishers Weekly,* 256,19, May, 26-30. 4p.

Dempsey, K. (2009). *The accidental library marketer.* Medford, NJ: Information Today.

Enis, M. (2012). Print control. *Library Journal,* 137, 12, Jul, 38-40.

Khan, M. (2008). *The library safety and security guide to prevention, planning, and response.* Chicago, IL: ALA.

Kumar, B. (2011). *What is the big deal with the "Big Deal"?* LibNotes. Retrieved from http://uccslib.org/libnotes/2011/08/24/whats-the-big-deal-with-the-big-deal/

McDermott, I. (2012). Silver Tech. *Searcher,* 20, 2, Mar, 7-11.

McDonell, C. (2007). Data mining for Library Media Centers. In J. Repman & G. K. Dickinson (Eds.), *School Library Management.* (6th ed.). Columbus, OH: Linworth Pub.

Neiburger, E. ((2007). *Gamers… in the library?!: the why, what, and how of videogame tournaments for all ages.* Chicago, IL: ALA.

Primary Research Group (2007). *Academic library websites benchmarks.* New York, NY: Primary Research Group.

Robbins, W. (2011). Baby Boomers, their elders and the Public Library. *Feliciter,* 57, 6, 233-234.

Roberts, A. & Smith, R. (2010). *Crash course in library services to people with disabilities.* Santa Barbara, CA: Libraries Unlimited.

Shon, S. (2006). How will this serve the community? Deciding who can speak at your library. *Public Libraries,* 45, 6 Nov/Dec, 8-13.

Solomon, L. (2011). *Doing social media so it matters: a librarian's guide.* Chicago, IL: ALA.

Stuart, D. (2012). *Technological threats to privacy and information access. School Library Journal.* 36, 5, Sep/Oct, 35-37.

USA Today, 06/25/(2012). Savvy seniors learn the ropes to use Facebook. *Money,* Jun 25, 02b.

Waters, A. (2011). The truth about tablets: educators are getting iPads and ereaders into students' hands – but it's not easy. *School Library Journal,* 58, 4, Apr, 36-38.

Zino, E. (2009). Let's fix virtual reference. *Library Journal,* Feb 1. Retrieved from http://www.libraryjournal.com/article/CA6631215.htm

PUBLIC LIBRARIES 3

Different types of public libraries receive funds from various sources, but the government continues to be a major contributor. Libraries need to fulfill requirements to receive money, provide open hours, and comply with regulations, such as on disabilities and computer filtering. Government support to public libraries are declining, due to tax payer resistance to tax increases, changes in population demographics and competition with other public services (Landau, 2008). According to the Institute of Museum and Library Services' 2010 Public Libraries Survey operating revenue funding percentages vary from state to state. The local government contributes 70–90% and the state 1–10% (Miller et. al., 2011). Property, excise and sales taxes, bonds, fees and fines, gifts and bequests are additional income sources (Turner, 2007). Friends of the Library, Library Foundations and grants can significant sources of income as well. ALA provides funding news updates on public libraries nationwide (http://www.ala.org/advocacy/libfunding/public).

Library Commissions or Board of Directors represent the interests of the community, serving as regulators of the library finances and staff. Coordination with the library director is essential to maintain the organization and keep it financially healthy and well administered. Library employees, Extra-Help Librarians included, are directly affected by these decision-makers. The policies and the yearly budget they pass result in work changes and even salaries. Libraries' policies state administrative regulations, including patrons' rights and responsibilities. Even during economic hardship, efforts are made to enable patrons to use libraries' facilities regardless of where they live. For example, those patrons not residing within local boundaries can use the library as a guest or a visitor. They may be required to show some form of identification, or perhaps none at all, to use in-house resources. But for remote access a library card is required.

A library's economic and political stability affects the quality and longevity of a job. To better understand an organization, it is useful to check on its revenues, expenditures, assets and liabilities. As far as the Extra-Help Librarians' budget, allocation is not always clearly stated and it might be combined with other categories. Public libraries' financial statements are obtainable, some of them even post it online, and this makes them easily accessible. A directory of public libraries can be a starting point to lead to more detailed information.

Organization

LIBRARY MISSIONS

Public libraries' coverage is quite extensive and their mission statements tend to encompass various points that define their purpose. Often they contain some of the aspects outlined below:

Nature: public service agency
Public: entire community residents of an area—neighborhood, city, county, etc.
Direct/Administer: Board of Trustees, staff
Groups served: adults, teenagers, young children, parents, elderly
Provide: resources and services (cost effective materials, programs, and technologies)
Collection: up to date, timely, accurate coverage of interests, needs and demands at the personal, professional, educational, cultural and recreational levels
Processes: select, acquire, organize and preserve books and other materials
Connection: reading and learning
Commitments: intellectual freedom, free and equal access, quality service
Values: be responsive, engage, encourage
Outreach: community work and diversity
Partnership and cooperation: libraries and other agencies
Facilities considerations: convenient, welcoming, safe

PUBLIC LIBRARY ISSUES

Many factors influence a public library's organization and services, involving issues that are of external and internal relevance. Some of these factors include the following:

- Decrease in funding
- Demand for services, such as computer and job search assistance
- Inclusiveness of the homeless and other underprivileged persons
- Balance between community needs versus collections acquisition
- Coverage of a diverse socio-economic and cultural population
- Community outreach limitations

- Partnership development with other entities
- Patrons' widespread age groups
- Literacy support

Extra-Help Librarians in public libraries can make a difference in staff support as they understand their organization's issues and complexities. In most of their assignments they work closely with the public, providing information and services. In this particular instance their performance should be recognized by administrators and factored into the resulting public support to the libraries as well.

ORGANIZATIONAL STRUCTURE

JOB POSITIONS

Professional experience, educational background (MLIS, Ph.D.), seniority and job responsibilities are aspects considered in each employment category. However, Extra-Help Librarians are not tied to seniority. In general, they are a group apart, composed of librarians from various categories, as presented on chapter 1. Therefore, the group is a mixture of different professional experiences, ages and goals. The categories below are included in the chain of command in a public library:

>Board of Directors or Library Commission
>Directors
>Department or Branch Managers
>Supervisors
>Librarian I, II, III, IV
>Library Assistant or Associate
>Librarian Extra-Help or Substitute

LIBRARY LOCATIONS

The size of a city, its various neighborhoods, its needs and finances determines the reach of a library or its library system. A small city library might be contained in one building. A metropolis may have extended jurisdiction over several communities, serving them at several places. Large library systems have layers of personnel with ample skills to manage the library. Consequently, physical space and personnel are basic factors in a library's structure. Libraries are organized as a single or as multiple units:

- Central Library
- Branch Library

- Rural Stations
- Bookmobile
- Central Library & Branches

There are physical, community and hierarchical differences between the main library and the branches. Extra-Help Librarians come to understand each place's subtleties as they spend time there and acquire experience. Working in the main library only, in branches, or in both, they learn unwritten information not found in the libraries' policies manual. Considerations on libraries space, staff and local characteristics in terms of patrons profile and collection needs, make each location unique and an attractive workplace.

Main libraries, as expected, are generally bigger and well staffed, the collection is broader and more services are available. Patrons are a diversity of people from the vicinity, city neighborhoods and out-of-town visitors. Therefore, it generally needs more staff and it also means that team work is even more necessary to make staff and patrons' interactions flow smoothly, particularly during busy times. Also, librarians have less frequent contact with the same person and Extra-Help Librarians are even less recognizable due to the infrequency in which they work there. The level of responsibility is usually lessened, because of the number of other librarians present and existence of various layers of personnel and responsibilities.

Branch libraries in a neighborhood or a small city have their own characteristics, too. The chances of knowing patrons and staff more closely are higher due to the smaller space, less staff and frequency of repeat patrons. Opportunities to work solo might happen in small branches and more responsibilities are often put upon Extra-Help Librarians in such occasions. For instance, even though there are procedures to follow, it can be stressful at times to do daily money count and branch closing. But it is rewarding to perform duties which normally are not part of Extra-Help Librarians' duties.

When working in the main library, or in a branch, it is important to know assigned responsibilities and quickly incorporate them to efficiently respond to patrons' needs. At public libraries patrons ask a variety of questions that range from simple directions to more complex information which might require further research. Extra-Help Librarians primary responsibility is to assist patrons at the reference desk. Most of the time assigned projects are performed alongside the face-to-face contact with patrons, unless the work needs to take place away from the desk.

Patrons

Each community has its own characteristics and their composition is influenced by economical and social factors. Communities differ in regards to their homogeneity level. Public libraries reflect their communities through the services they provide. Collections and programs are adapted to suit patrons' needs and draw their participation. The patrons' profile encompasses a wide range of age groups and social and economic statuses.

In this context, Extra-Help Librarians work requires broad knowledge of adults, children and young adults' collections and other services. When working in specific areas or information desks, children or adult, it is helpful to know about patrons' behavior and scheduled activities or programs for each age group. A variety of services are offered and some of them have become a tradition. Summer reading, holiday events and other children's activities are examples of a public library's presence in the community.

CHILDREN

Babies, preschoolers and elementary school children are curious beings, but they can be reserved when interacting with strangers. Parents or caregivers accompany the children to the library to check out books for reading or research purposes. They often ask for reading recommendations for specific grade levels and a school's reading lists. Some of them motivate the child to ask the librarian for what they need while others take the primary role. Students frequently request information on subjects they are studying or doing school research on.

Library usage in the children's area changes as the day progresses. In the morning it receives mostly parents with their babies and preschoolers. Most of the activities are geared to these groups. After school libraries are hectic with students and their parents. They often need a lot of attention from librarians to gather resources that usually supplement their school library's collection.

Extra-Help Librarians learn family behavior patterns, reading and research needs of the young, as well as the activities offered as they work in a community. Literature knowledge of the classics, book awards and series and reading level recommendations are of important. It is also useful to know monthly children's activities. A calendar might be available in print or online. Specific details about each program, volunteer involvement, the sign-up process and any rewards or prizes should be available. Examples of very popular programs are included in the next page:

- Summer reading program
- After school activities
- Puppet shows
- Storytimes

YOUNG ADULT

An increasing allocation of space and of dedicated librarians to develop collections, programs and other services for young adults (YA) are some indicators that these patrons are receiving more attention from libraries. Such initiative may generate more involved adults in libraries in the near future. Newer librarians are definitely bringing more knowledge and enthusiasm to the YA area and encountering more support from library administrators. Even though Extra-Help Librarians do not have the opportunity to work with only one group of patrons in public libraries, they do get a fair amount of exposure to each one. So, there are chances to interact with YA patrons, learn about their collection and observe their behavior patterns.

That said, Extra-Help Librarians' work with young adults can often include informing them on volunteer programs, upcoming events and collection materials. For instance, graphic novels are in a genre of high demand and it leads readers to other sections, such as how to draw Manga. Also, knowing their behavior patterns is important. Giving them time to browse for what they need on their own before approaching them is sometimes wise. Other issues to be aware of when interacting with young adults are:

- Peer connection
- High level of technology use
- Sullen or introverted behavior
- Challenge to rules and can be disruptive

A sensible approach to young adults perhaps requires a bit more repetition, persistence and argumentation. Overall, teenagers come to public libraries to do homework research, use the computer, hang out after school and spend time with friends among other reasons. Extra-Help Librarians' should be prepared to support such needs by knowing about the materials' content and location, library behavior procedures and resources. Knowledge about their behavior, expectations and emotions can facilitate interactions with them.

It is not uncommon to have to work with parents when young adults need materials for school assignments. Deadlines are often short, sometimes next day, and this can prevent access to materials not on site. In such cases, it becomes the perfect opportunity to introduce databases to their mix of research tools. Then, online resources—instead of being a supplement—become the only option.

Programs aimed to young adults are planned to entertain, give them opportunity to express themselves and to develop a sense of community. Examples of programs of interest are:

- Movie and game nights
- Poetry slams
- Reading clubs

It is relevant to mention that the increasing number of YA librarians has been important to the development of programs and the collections geared to this group. The support that Extra-Help Librarians can give to permanent staff working in this area is mutually beneficial.

ADULTS

The majority of library materials acquired are for adult use. Many activities are planned to meet their needs and keep them engaged and returning for more. Adult patrons have a variety of interests and that is very challenging for public libraries. There are so many subjects to cover, limited space to accommodate them and limited amount of money to acquire them. Nonetheless, libraries in metropolitan areas and small communities manage to obtain resources of significance to their patrons. New book releases, dvd's and magazines are some of the formats in demand.

Public services such as computer access, tax help and others are highly useful to the adult community in particular. Programs are also offered, some seasonal and others on-going, depending on staff time and financial resources. The list below represents some of the many well-liked programs public libraries offer:

- Book discussion groups
- Internet classes
- Gardening workshops
- Musical presentations
- Art Shows

Extra-Help Librarians interpersonal skills are of key importance when working with adults. While most of them are polite and well meaning people there are other patrons who can be difficult. Public libraries are desirable places to work, but a simplistic approach can be deceiving. It is necessary to understand that they serve a diverse population and it is a workplace that might require more heartiness and hardness than other types of libraries. That is in addition to the demands that the Extra-Help Librarian category entails. Adult patrons often lack the spiritual and physical grace that we associate with children and young adults.

Library Responsibilities & Library Services

COLLECTION

Communities have their own characteristics and library needs. Therefore, collections must have some fundamental materials useful for any community and also include additional subjects and formats that are necessary in a specific community. There are a few collection organization methods and most public and school libraries use the numeral based Dewey Decimal System (DDC). Some have implemented alternative methods. Dewey's classification knowledge areas are divided in classes and subdivisions that aim to make it easier to find materials. Librarians' ability to find the library's materials requires experience in using the catalog and knowing where the items are physically located. Consequently, Extra-Help Librarians—mainly those without previous library experience or not familiar with the collection and their location in the building—need to practice search strategies to quickly locate materials for patrons. Also, a consideration of a library's size and its customer service approach to show patrons where the items are, helps them comprehend Dewey's organization and their location at the library. After awhile, frequently used sections might be remembered automatically. This can factor into patrons becoming more confident searchers.

In addition, libraries have developed directional and identification tools to help patrons find materials. Signs placed on various sections and labels on materials give patrons information to identify areas and materials with ease. Such guides also orientate Extra-Help Librarians, especially when space is reorganized, sections are moved and other changes have been introduced since the last time they worked in that library. In such cases, manager or other staff should communicate any changes before the library opens to the public, giving Extra-Help Librarians time to imprint the current placement of the collection. It can be challenging to know all about the collection placement, in particular for Extra-Help Librarians that cover more than one library and one area.

Public library collections encompass many sections and subsections. The literature can be divided by language and genres, separated or interfiled. The structural organization of materials—in fiction and non-fiction; print and media (audiobooks, cd's, dvd's, cd-rom); hardcover or paperbacks; oversize; newspapers and magazines—might seem difficult to locate for patrons that are not regular users. Acknowledging this, Extra-Help Librarians should be aware that they need to be familiar with patrons' needs and the collection organization to direct patrons and fulfill their requests.

Collection labels are used as materials identifiers, beneficial to patrons and Extra-Help Librarians alike and some are more frequently used than others.

Labels commonly used are:

- Library name stamp and branch stickers
- Dewey Decimal number
- Reference materials
- Author names
- Genre stickers

Other materials are shelved in sections with identifying codes according to the categories illustrated in the table below:

Materials Type	Abbreviation
Picture Books	E
Early Readers	R or ER
Science Fiction	SF
Adult Fiction	F
Mystery	M
Spanish	SP
Graphic Novels	GF
Young Adult	YA or Y
Biographies	B

Table No. 3.1. Collection Code Abbreviations

The location of various materials that might not be directly visible or easily accessible to patrons include accelerated reading lists, school reading lists, grade lists, desk reference materials and more. They might not be used as often as other items and Extra-Help Librarians have to revisit their location to be able to know where they are when needed. On the other hand, patrons ask about items that are used frequently and they include the following high demand materials:

- Fiction
- DVD's
- Travel guidebooks
- Legal matters
- Landscaping
- Biographies
- Language
- Cookbooks & diet

PROGRAMS & ACTIVITIES

The planning process of library programming can be long due to theme selection, scheduling and approval. Extra-Help Librarians are generally involved in programs' promotion phases, but support during preparation and execution is not uncommon. Check the library's calendar of events daily to remind patrons of upcoming community events. Libraries program events free of charge, such as music shows, art exhibits and crafts activities, to attract patrons to the library, providing enjoyment and enrichment. Programs in general create opportunities to increase circulation.

The Summer Reading program is the longest program in public libraries. Usually, Extra-Help Librarians working at the children' desk will be involved with parts of it, such as the sign-up for children or the distribution of weekly prizes and incentives. Storytime and after school programmed activities might be other responsibilities, depending on professional experience and interest and the library's need.

READERS ADVISORY

Patrons often ask for suggestions on what to read next. Extra-Help Librarians who are strong readers and literature lovers are most certainly pleased to take this task. Others might have to use a variety of strategies to provide an effective readers' advisory service. During the reference interview, find out about what the person has read or which genres they enjoy. In general, recommendations are based on patrons' personal reading preferences. Use personal and online book lists or specific databases as needed. In case the library subscribes to databases like Literature Online or NoveList, introduce it to the patron for further use. Familiarity with a few publication lists on various genres will make suggestions an easier process. Suggest a few favorite reads of your own, keep a list of classics, bestsellers or great reads. Take advantage of read alike books and guide patrons to discussion groups lists.

Professional organizations also maintain recommended reading lists for adults, young adults and children. There are libraries that publish their own reading lists for teens and children, even by grade level. Even when in lack of a strong readers' advisory background, Extra-Help Librarians have lots of chances to learn quickly. Many books are requested regularly, classics and bestsellers in particular. A library's new acquisitions list is a source of good reads. Sign up for e-mail notifications or regularly check the library website for lists of new materials.

Even though readers' advisory is traditionally associated with fiction materials there are many adults who prefer to read non-fiction. Travel journals, biographies and memoirs are frequently in demand. Non-fiction bestsellers list sources might contribute to Extra-Help Librarians personal suggestions to patrons.

BOOK DISCUSSION

Literature lovers who enjoy exchanging their perceptions of selected books gather at public libraries in structured groups or informally with friends and acquaintances. There are many established adult book discussion groups focusing generally on fiction, mystery and non-fiction. Children and parents' book discussion groups tend be flexible on their reading preferences, depending on the child's sex, age, grade level and interests.

Even though Extra-Help Librarians might not be responsible to lead the groups, it is of importance to be informed about upcoming gatherings dates, which is the book of the month and where copies are kept for distribution. Usually the book of choice is available at the time the group meets for the current month discussion. If a group participant misses the meeting or a patron wants to join the group it is best to be prepared to provide the book and meeting details. It is also useful to know how to locate lists of books discussed in the past and perhaps even have read some of them.

External book groups, not sponsored by the library, can select their book from the library's reading list. In this case, there is a need to know how to locate these lists and the procedures to acquire them for interested groups. In short assignments, it is recommended to pass to the librarian in charge the steps taken and the information of the books requestor for follow up.

NON-ENGLISH & BILINGUAL SERVICES

Historically, libraries in metropolitan areas have built collections in various languages in response to their patrons' needs. In more recent years, smaller communities have increasingly been impacted by a flow of newcomers from various parts of the world. The reasons are often related to world conflicts, international policies and immigration laws. Effects are felt in local economies and library services. In the midst of changes, libraries react as support to immigrants and established patrons that speak languages other than English.

Communities with such characteristics have demand for librarians who can communicate in a foreign language. These skills facilitate clear communication with patrons about the library's resources at their disposal. An Extra-Help Librarian's knowledge of patrons' languages, customs and understanding—and respect for patrons' difficulties in their new environment—makes the interaction productive. It is even more critical for those professionals without such skills to know the non-English materials general content, location, catalog search strategies and the library's website in other languages. Familiarity with the community and the library policies are other important aspects that make contact with patrons more successful.

The library strategic plan takes in account the community mix and delineates areas of action to serve patrons appropriately. When plans are implemented, the needs of communities with a high percentage of non-English speakers are likely to be supported with a wider range of resources. Extra-Help Librarians should inform patrons about available services to increase awareness, participation and usage. The following resources are examples of libraries' efforts to reach non-English speakers.

LIBRARY WEBSITES OR WEBPAGES

Libraries serving diverse communities tend to offer information in more than one language in their website. Content is made available through a complete non-English version or is limited to certain webpages. Library funding, community size and bilingual or multilingual personnel determine the extent of the content. Access to the catalog in other languages is an advantage to those patrons who function better in their first language by need or choice.

COMMUNITY INFORMATION FOR NON-ENGLISH SPEAKERS

Information in languages other than English is also available at libraries in various formats and from many sources. Newspapers of foreign or local sources, community and library calendars of events, English as Second Language (ESL) classes or tutoring through literacy leagues and other providers, ethnic group meetings, United States citizenship resources (such as test books or immigration information) and other items are usually ready for distribution to interested patrons and visitors. It is useful to patrons to have access to information in their specific languages, enabling them to find the needed resources on their own.

BILINGUAL & ETHNIC EVENTS

Other ways libraries are reaching out to those that speak languages other than English include programs such as bilingual storytimes, activities celebrating other countries' customs, ethnic music and dance shows. Basic bilingual computer instruction might also be offered to older patrons.

Some of the steps to reach Latinos, for example, include knowing the community, developing collections and services, translation of handouts, marketing, staff involvement, partnerships and use of technology in outreach efforts (Ocón, 2006). These strategies are valuable to any community with foreign language needs.

FOREIGN LANGUAGE COLLECTION

Foreign Language Materials

Books have usually been the main format in foreign language collections. It takes time to be able to develop a quality collection, requiring funds for acquisition, professional's knowledge of targeted languages and the development of relationships with vendors. Attendance to publishers' fairs is another opportunity that allows purchase of materials in other formats, such as in audio or video.

Multilingual Materials

Many multilingual materials, written in two or more languages, are generally designed for children. Adults also take advantage of these materials to learn or teach another language—teachers and parents for instance. Library systems are more likely to have uniform foreign materials labels, tags and such, but self-contained libraries usually decide individually where items are shelved. When a collection in a particular language has a high quantity of items, they can be found in a section of their own, most likely adult or children. Otherwise, without due caution, items might be interfiled with English materials. Adequate item labeling, library signs and shelvers training makes it easier for shelvers to put them in the accurate location and for patrons to find them.

REFERRALS

Libraries routinely provide referrals to other persons and entities. Extra-Help Librarians are acquainted with the fact that referrals require knowledge of the local community. The challenge is more accentuated when they work in various libraries. However, a library's local resources binder or the community area can contain substantial information. Online searches often offer up-to-date information for date sensitive matters. Requests for referrals can involve:

- Tax help assistance
- Tutoring services
- Literacy programs
- Museums and Archives
- Other libraries (academic, special)
- Non-profit organizations
- Community events
- Grant related resources

Other services provided, and details on some of the most commonly requested referrals, are presented below. Note that there is a vast quantity of referrals that are not mentioned. Each library prioritizes the services that it provides considering community needs, funds, personnel and for other reasons. Extra-Help Librarians in direct contact with patron will have responsibilities related to the services that are selectively introduced here.

TAX FORMS

Some libraries annually partner with the Internal Revenue Service (IRS) in the Tax Forms Outlets Program (TFOP) to make tax forms available to patrons usually from the end of January to April. Extra-Help Librarians are likely to be involved in the process keeping track of available forms and replenishing them. In addition, they frequently direct patrons to the forms, provide referrals to organizations in the area that provide tax assistance to low income individuals and search for and print forms not available at the library.

Throughout the year there are individuals that seek tax forms. Often libraries keep binders of reproducible tax forms for the current and previous years and patrons can make photocopies of the ones they need. There are some forms that the IRS does not make available in print. These tax forms can be downloaded from the IRS website. The ultimate resource for further questions is the IRS toll free number.

Since tax time is intense for a few months of the years, Extra-Help Librarians need training or reminders of the changes and procedures in place for the current year. Updates on form delays and shortages are especially important so they can respond accurately to patrons' inquiries. It is useful to know where the reproducible tax forms binder is kept for easy access when needed. Libraries still are one of the few outlets for tax forms and related information. Even though this service is provided for a short period of time, it impacts the library and patrons. Libraries offer a service that has demand and generates a high influx of patrons. They in turn have easy access to the tax forms and other materials.

ARCHIVES

Museums, history rooms and archives are some of the most common places for historical and genealogical research. On the other hand, it is not unusual to find libraries that incorporate some of them as part of their organization. When that is not the case they are frequently used as referral to materials that are not in the scope of the library's collection.

Patrons tracing family history, researchers interested in local history and visitors in general are some of the people interested in history and archival collections at libraries. An Extra-Help Librarian's knowledge of photographs, school yearbooks, city directories and even genealogy databases can facilitate patrons access to the information they seek.

Libraries also house historic or recent newspaper records in microfilm format. Local newspapers in particular are a source of family members' obituaries. Libraries often provide this service and Extra-Help Librarians can coach patrons on microfilm's usage and how to fill out obituary requests. They inform out-of-town requestors about the procedures to obtain the information or point them to the library website to get more details. These requests are filled depending on staff time and in some libraries often without charge.

Genealogy research is complex, requiring more time and detailed instruction and specialists in this area provide the best results. Extra-Help Librarians should be able to demonstrate the basic features of genealogy databases the library subscribes. When the library does not offer access to such resources, refer patrons to other institutions that do or can assist them further.

HOMESCHOOLING & TUTORING

Parents that opt to homeschool their children are frequent users of public libraries. They have a diversity of interests and needs. They often use the library to supplement educational materials, asking for resources and reading suggestions. Besides, the library is a welcoming place that offers knowledgeable staff and a wide range of activities to children and families. The library can be a support system for families' goals for their children's education.

Tutors also use the library space to conduct their business. Tutors are usually connected to a literacy organization or are private teachers. Connections between the library and these groups differ. Partnerships with literacy leagues are common since both organizations are linked to literacy goals. Private teachers regularly use the library space to conduct their business. The relationship is informal without any inquiry into these tutors' activities. Some library systems develop a special literacy collection and might even have study areas, especially if they have their own literacy program.

Extra-Help Librarians might be able to identify these groups as they work often in a library frequented by homeschoolers and tutors. It is good to know their needs, subject areas of interest in the collections and requirements involved in reserving study rooms. If that is the case, it is necessary to check the calendar for the day's schedule to avoid conflicts with previous reservations.

TECHNOLOGY MANAGEMENT

Local patrons and out-of-town visitors are frequent users of libraries' computers and the WiFi connection. The 2011–2012 Study of the Public Library Funding & Technology Access (Hoffman, Bertot, & Davis, 2012) states that 65 percent of the libraries reported shortage in public computers to meet demand and 91 percent of them provide free WiFi. This indicates libraries importance to patrons' technology needs. Considering this context, librarians interact with patrons to connect them to computers, instruct them on how to access the internet and the library's online resources. Informally or through planned workshops, technology instruction focuses on basic computer tools, overview of relevant websites and domains, information accuracy and personal data safety.

Extra-Help Librarians also perform the aforementioned responsibilities to a certain degree. Assistance to patrons' catalog search, e-mail access and word processing difficulties often involve handling patrons' frustrations. Knowledge of a library's internet usage policy, as well as WiFi connection access, makes handling computer problems more manageable. The problems in these areas happen repeatedly with many opportunities to handle them.

TECHNOLOGY ASSISTANCE SCENARIOS

Before the library opens to the public Extra-Help Librarians might be in charge of manually turning computers on if technicians are not available to do the task or if computers are not timed to turn on automatically. On an ongoing basis Extra-Help Librarians manage all kinds of technical problems when helping patrons.

Public computer access attracts patrons with regular and sporadic needs. Patrons without computers at home come to the library to use their hardware and software for many reasons, including the set-up of e-mail accounts, the checking of them, writing resumes, searching for products and services, paying bills, doing school work and playing games. Patrons who occasionally have problems with their home computer hardware or online connection use the library's computer to check their e-mail and print documents. Out-of-town guests also check e-mail, get online map directions and print airplane reservations.

It is also part of the duties to report on hardware failure and follow up instructions from technical support. Overall, Extra-Help Librarians troubleshooting skills is desirable to handle at least minor technical problems, mainly when the department of technology is off-site and staff is limited. Staff technology support depends on the size of the library and the computer services provided to patrons.

COMPUTER FILTERS

Libraries computers are used for many purposes, even to link to inappropriate websites. Uncontrolled access to pornography, in particular, heads the debate over the use of filters in public libraries computers. Filters are installed to prevent patrons' access to these sources. Controversies focus on patrons' rights to access any websites, regardless of the content. Laws at Federal, State, and local level regulate the usage of filtering software, but there are libraries that opt out of compliance, meaning that they are not eligible to receive some government funds.

Library policies specify how privacy issues are handled. Libraries that do not use filters might implement preventive measures. Space design places computers on locations that allow patrons to have more privacy and computer screens covers are made available to limit public viewing. Extra-Help Librarians familiarity with library policies, strategies on how to proceed when confronted with patrons' complaints and provision of protective screens to patrons might prove necessary.

Public libraries are diverse institutions geared to serve people with all kinds of interest. Extra-Help Librarians have the opportunity to apply their skills in contrasting situations. They also can learn from the experiences at the personal and professional level.

CHAPTER REFERENCES

American Library Association (2013). *Public Libraries funding updates.* Retrieved from http://www.ala.org/advocacy/libfunding/public

Hoffman, J., Bertot, J. & Davis, D. (2012). Libraries Connect Communities: Public Library Funding & Technology Access Study 2011-2012. *American Libraries.* Jun. Retrieved from http://viewer.zmags.com/publication/4673a369#/4673a369/1

Miller, K., Swan, D., Craig, T., Dorinski, S., Freeman, M., Isaac, N., O'Shea, P., Schilling, P., Scotto, J., (2011). *Public Libraries Survey: Fiscal Year 2009* (IMLS-2011–PLS-02). Institute of Museum and Library Services. Washington, DC. Retrieved from https://harvester.census.gov/imls/pubs/Publications/pls2009.pdf

Landau, H. (2008). *The small public library survival guide: thriving on less.* Chicago, IL: ALA.

Ocón, B. (2006). 10 steps for effective outreach to the latino community. In G. M. Eberhart (Ed.), *The whole library handbook 4.* Chicago, IL: ALA.

Turner, A. M. (2007). *Managing money: a guide for librarians.* Jefferson, NC: McFarland & Co.

ACADEMIC LIBRARIES 4

Higher Education institutions have their own intricacies, but there are similarities of purpose and mission, structural governance and accreditation requirements. Some of the aspects that differentiate them are generally the provenience of funds and the programs offered. A brief synopsis of the educational system is presented to comprehend how the university library fits in that framework. The institutional structure will be shown from the top down, narrowing it to librarian category levels and responsibilities. In due course the focus is on Extra-Help Librarians in relation to academic library staff needs and services provided to patrons.

Emphasis is put on Extra-Help Librarians' practice and need for continuing update on technology, especially when their responsibilities include information literacy instruction. New librarian graduates are bound to be more comfortable with the current use of technology and are more familiar with specific tools. Librarian Extra-Help's learning curve will depend also on their age, personal needs and inquisitiveness. Overall, considering the ever changing nature of technology and it's expanding features, and in many cases company consolidations, products mentioned here and currently in the market will continue to be relevant and useful to librarians.

Organization

Higher Education includes various types of institutions, such as colleges and universities. The Carnegie Foundation for the Advancement of Teaching has created, and enhanced over the years, The Carnegie Classification of Institutions of Higher Education (http://classifications.carnegiefoundation.org/). This organizes institutions into groups according to a range of similarities and differences. You can access them using the following classifications: Basic, Undergraduate and Graduate Instructional Program, Enrollment Profile and Undergraduate Profile, and Size & Setting. Such listings provide clear information about how academic institutions interrelate at defined levels.

Libraries are part of a range of academic institutions such as Research Universities, Private Universities, State Universities, City, Community or Junior Colleges and Technical Institutes. These offer degrees and programs for undergraduates and graduates, Certificates Programs, Lifelong Programs/Continuing Education, Online Learning/Distance Education, work/study abroad and others. Therefore, academic libraries differ on their goals, student bodies and approaches to services.

JOB STRUCTURE

Personnel matters can also be complex, spreading over a variety of tiers depending on the institution and its size. At the library level personnel distributions cover staffs in different functions and responsibilities, as follow:

> Library Dean
> Librarian Supervisors/Department Managers
> Librarians: Reference, Instruction, Department Liaison, Technical Services
> Librarian Adjunct Pool
> Circulation
> Student Aids/Workers

Adjunct Pool Librarians are designated here as Extra-Help Librarians. The term switch is used to give a more uniform treatment to the subjects discussed. Considering that academic institutions use Adjunct Pool for other workers categories, such as professors, it is fundamental that this practicality is understood since it aims to expand on the concepts of previous chapters.

That explained, Extra-Help Librarians' work can encompass generalist and specialist skills. Unless the institution states it's need for specific area skills—such as reference or instruction—it is usually assumed that the position search focus is on generalists' skills. However, they can also be subject specialists trained to work in a specific area, such as teaching. The Extra-Help Librarians pool includes professionals with background in other types of libraries as well, making it a diverse mix of experiences. The needs of the library in areas such as reference, research and instruction can influence the composition of the group.

LIBRARIAN BENEFITS

Various factors influence the rewards offered to academic librarians. It depends on individual institution's structure, policies and financial stability to be able, or not, to provide benefits to this category.

In general terms academic librarians' compensation package for full-time and regular part-time faculty often includes:

- Salary
- Sabbatical leaves
- Promotion
- Tuition wavers
- Travel allowances
- Paid conferences participation
- Access to campus sports facilities
- Medical and vision benefits

Proportional benefits are awarded to regular part-time employees. Extra-Help Librarians receive earnings based on the total number of hours worked or an estimate of those. For example, Extra-Help Librarians instructors are compensated for a fixed number of hours per course, regardless of how many hours it takes to plan the course and design materials, as well as assist students and grade their work. The Academic Affairs Department and the institution's employee benefits webpage offer some indication about compensation. Participation in academic librarian listservs can also add to the understanding of such issues, since participants are more prone to share their experience from different institutions.

Extra-Help Librarians are not subjected to the same level of a faculty librarian's expectations and regulations in regards to others academic aspects of the profession, for example:

- Research and publish work
- Acquisition of job security through tenure status
- Participation on committees and professional conferences
- Pursuance of library liaison responsibilities

These points are raised to clarify employment limitations of Extra-Help Librarians compared to responsibilities and compensations available to full-time librarians. This may be relevant to those who want to pursue a career in academic libraries. Starting as an Extra-Help Librarian can lead into other permanent positions, but chances are reduced compared to public libraries, for instance. The level of experience necessary is higher since "there are no entry-level jobs at academic libraries" (Neely, 2011). The knowledge of academic reference, teaching and instruction tools makes entry into a pool more challenging. In addition, there is an abundance of databases and study areas. Also, academic libraries often open their Extra-Help Librarians pool, but are conservative in using it. Since the application and hiring process can take even months, the institution's needs for this category are frequently not met with demand exceeding supply. Other library types use the same strategies. Due to the nature of the position, it is clear that being in a Extra-Help Librarians' pool does not mean that there will be assignments. However, it is not uncommon to be in an academic pool for years and rarely get work. At times there is even a need to reapply.

New Extra-Help Librarians can be overwhelmed in the beginning with so much to learn about the institution and subject matters. Instructors, for instance, confront a steep technology learning curve and, even with training, it is worthwhile to weigh the amount of time invested into teaching and the financial rewards from it, which can be surprisingly moderate.

LIBRARY LOCATIONS

The changing academic environment is apparent with the diversification of the campuses locations as the list below illustrates:

- Main University campus
- Satellite campus
- Same campus, various libraries
- Online branch

These various locations require different library's strategies. Considering that many study areas are less dependent on the location of universities and colleges, libraries are expanding their focus. In addition to in-library services, there are also increasing demands for digital access services. With students and faculty accessing libraries from widespread time zones, libraries create and maintain resources that can be utilized from anywhere. Location is becoming less relevant but librarians work demands are escalating. As a consequence, the amount of a librarians' daily work, new projects development, staff training and more generates the need for Extra-Help Librarians.

ACADEMIC LIBRARIES ISSUES

The Association of Colleges and Research Libraries reports on academic library issues, covering aspects of professional concerns and trends. Libraries role, librarians' recruitment, digital creation and preservation and information technology (Hisle, 2002; ACRL Research Planning and Review Committee, 2010) are recurring topics. Other practical samples of the many issues are listed below:

- Institution accreditation
- Learning technologies
- Consortium participation
- Learning styles
- E-Learning

- Tenure and peer review
- Relevance of primary sources and metadata
- Open Access depositories
- Faculty and librarian relations
- Information Literacy Standards

- Tutorials and handouts
- Instruction surveys
- Plagiarism
- Federated searching
- Google Scholar and databases
- ILL: resources and limitations
- Popular and scholarly resources
- Citation styles
- Journal subscription high costs
- Collection digitization
- Online resources 24/7
- Library orientation to freshman, parents, new employees, faculty

Extra-Help Librarians need to be aware of such issues and update and expand their knowledge about the organization to better serve their users. Especially because Extra-Help Librarians work in a variety of areas, it is critical that they are attentive to evolving and new academic issues. Besides, when opportunities to move to other positions arise, the accumulated knowledge might play an essential role in the process.

POTENTIAL PROBLEMS

Awareness of problems that often happen or might happen at work can make a difference on outcomes. Discussions of various scenarios during training, focusing on types of situations, what to do, when to act and who to contact can be critical. Guidelines on such matters are found in policies and procedures and an Extra-Help Librarians must know how to react or where the "employee handbook" is with necessary information. Therefore, keep it accessible just in case there is a need to verify how to proceed when faced with unfamiliar occurrences. Over longer assignments in particular, such as filling in for a vacancy or for a maternity leave, there are more chances to observe other librarians managing situations that require intervention and more back up for managing problems such as:

- Document deliveries
- Recall of materials
- Circulation and reserves
- Study rooms or community room reservation
- Emergencies
- Copyrights
- Vandalism
- Disruptive behavior
- Sexual offenses/harassment
- Misuse of study areas
- Materials accessibility

Security Levels: Campus & Buildings

Campuses usually have a workforce of their own to keep vigilance over it. Usually there is a police station that oversees parking, outbuildings and open areas. When it comes to intervening in occurrences taking place inside the library buildings, librarians have a direct connection with the campus police station to request any intervention over fights, thefts and other major problems. Beyond that, minor confrontations are handled directly by librarians. It is critical for Extra-Help Librarians to be observant of the different types of circumstances and applicable actions to take whenever problems emerge, report any incidents and keep the staff informed. Also, they should keep clear written records.

Depending on the size of the building and the access to the collection, there may be security tools in locations that permit broader vigilance over patrons and library assets. Clear visibility of the shelves is one of the major factors in security. In multilevel libraries, there are even more difficulty in overseeing areas and that can facilitate theft and users misbehavior. Increased staff visibility and walks through the shelves are a strategy combination used to reduce undesirable occurrences.

Main telephone numbers to have easy access to:

- Campus police
- Fire department
- Head librarian/supervisor

Patrons

Academic library patrons' characteristics change as institutions add new certificates, programs and classes, either on-campus or online. This promotes a wider group of patrons in terms of age, as well as computer and information literacy levels. Patrons belong to the following groups:

- Students
- Faculty
- Staff
- Local and global community

Librarians create and maintain services to these patrons, factoring in their location, needs and available funds. Each of them differs in the way they access the library and face-to-face contact is often secondary. Even those on-campus utilize various ways to access library materials. Learning their needs has become a more elaborate task. This relies even more on statistical data and the patrons' willingness to express criticism and suggestions in this new environment. In-library behavior observation is no longer a highly representative method to identify user needs.

Extra-Help Librarians staying current on these matters makes them better prepared to assist the clientele and support staff. For instance, the institution's extent of borrowing privileges given to their local community differs among academic libraries, indicating the range of their services. Also, know how to help patrons access online services and how to solve related problems. There are other functions of relevance that are institution specific. This can make the categories' work a challenge, but engaging.

STUDENTS

Higher Education institutions have a large number of young students. However, over the recent economic downturn older adults have invested in furthering their education, adding to the diversification of the student body. Reference and instructional librarians' work plans take in consideration the students' characteristics to provide services to meet the assessed needs. Extra-Help Librarians follow previously set coordinates when interacting with library patrons who often include native English speakers and foreign students, student workers and student volunteers. Tasks and approaches differ when in contact with each group, making it necessary to learn about each one.

NATIVE ENGLISH SPEAKERS

These students have a lot in common as far as school experience because they pretty much went through similar educational paths, except for home schooled and independent study students. Traditionally, library services have been geared to native English speakers. However, the focus is expanding due to globalization and new technology advancements, introducing new factors for consideration. For instance, Long Distance Education brings together a more heterogeneous group of students whose common language is English. This leads library support to be redesigned to accommodate native English speaker and other groups' needs.

INTERNATIONAL STUDENTS

Awareness of the difference of libraries in other countries, the existence or lack of services, rules and procedures about access to materials and knowledge of a student's language are taken into account to better guide international students in their new environment. Understanding the complexities involved and the student's background and needs, facilitates interactions and the promotion of better services to them and ultimately improves effectiveness of library usage.

Command of English varies among international students and unfamiliarity with library terminology and definitions can deter them from taking advantage of the services available. Library tours and new student orientation have been crucial opportunities to inform students, especially foreign students. They can provide basic explanations about library organization, resources and services. Information literacy and research classes help them further their library knowledge. Overall, outreach initiatives are necessary to engage international students in the library.

MULTICULTURAL STUDENTS

Cultural experiences set this group of students apart in many cases. Factors such as speaking English as a Second Language or other language issues can play a part. In addition, even when they are born in this country their parents came from other parts of the world and instilled in their children cultural values from their native country. Adoption and intercultural marriages also factor in when delineating services and strategies offered to students with diverse backgrounds.

STUDENT WORKERS & VOLUNTEERS

Libraries count largely on the support of paid and unpaid students with shelving, circulation and computer labs responsibilities. Extra-Help Librarians, especially those working in the evenings and weekends, might have to supervise student workers and volunteers. Clear knowledge of their tasks, expectations and routines makes the interaction positive and productive.

FACULTY

Extra-Help Librarians contact with faculty might not be frequent. But when working on the reference desk or in a collaborative project it is necessary to know how to access their contact information and the websites of those who have it. Faculty office hours, class schedules and committee participation can be another type of information requested by patrons. On-campus and off-campus faculty have different connections with the library. As an Extra-Help Librarian, on-campus and off-campus teaching responsibilities are possible and worth consideration.

ON-CAMPUS

Limited building space on-campus makes it difficult to provide offices for all faculties, but many professors have designated room offices. Their relationship with the library often depends on the class they teach, the materials they need and the projects they assign to their students. It is to their benefit that the library is close to them, even though that does not always make a substantial difference. Librarians might see such proximity as a step closer to getting to know faculty better and to develop alliances and work collaborations.

In another group, faculty teaching in-class short courses, either week days or weekends in particular, spend less time in-location and often do not hold an office on campus. That can lead to sporadic library use for them, limiting librarians' contact with these faculties.

OFF-CAMPUS

Online classes have changed libraries ways of providing services to students and also to faculty. Now, even semester long courses can be taught from anywhere by professors. They can also be taught by adjunct instructors from other campuses and institutions or by retired or new faculty. They can perform their responsibilities as telecommuters. Online teaching is a major advantage to faculty because it offers location flexibility. Librarians have to adjust to this new environment and set new strategies to reach faculty and to develop a relationship without direct contact.

Extra-Help Librarians can be part of either one of these groups. They provide reference on-campus libraries and/or teach off-campus classes. It depends on the needs of the library and not on compartmentalized hiring procedures. For this category, it would be to libraries disadvantage to establish hiring based on just a current and specific need.

STAFF

All of the institutions personnel are potential library patrons, regardless of the position they hold. It is a widespread group with needs that are not necessarily the academic library's goal to fulfill. For instance, their reading for pleasure needs might be fulfilled by the nearby public library or through interlibrary loans in some cases. That is because fiction collections are not top priority in academic libraries or other patrons' interest beyond the collection parameters.

LOCAL & GLOBAL COMMUNITIES

Services and access available to local and global communities are very distinct. Local communities can take advantage of various services that libraries offer on-campus. Lectures and art exhibits are most likely open to the public, welcoming local visitors. Collection use in the building is allowed, but check out is limited as stated in the library's policies. Global communities access the library's website, check the catalog, tutorials and subject guides. Only those holding the library's card are able to use the databases, download books and other resources.

Librarian Responsibilities

Reference and instruction are intrinsically interrelated and librarians might work in both areas or in just one. As institutions provide information literacy to students, librarians' functions acquire a more multifaceted mix. Small institutions lead librarians to spread their time over several work areas. In bigger libraries, it normally happens that librarians have more specific duties. Librarians' responsibilities are set according to the needs of the institution, reflection on other library workers as well.

Extra-Help Librarians have the responsibility to be well informed about the campus schools, departments and library services to students, faculty and staff in general. It is clearly overwhelming and they usually have a steep learning curve in the beginning. But time, continuing observation, practice using resources (especially databases), visits to other buildings (schools, administration, gymnasium, cafeteria, student union) and even walks in and around the campus result in increased knowledge and confidence.

Even though Extra-Help Librarians are limited in the scope of what they have a chance to do, the impact is nonetheless present. Their duties include coverage of assigned areas for certain periods, filling in for short or long durations, teaching information literacy classes and supporting students' research needs. Due to the specificity of each institution's delegation of work load, the focus here is therefore broad, aiming to give an overview of what constitutes Extra-Help Librarians' functions in an academic setting. Generally responsibilities involve:

- Reference service: face-to-face
- E-reference: e-mail, chats
- Instruction

Extra-Help Librarians are often involved directly in these areas. The circumstances that determine the assignments, duration and work needs, also determine how extensively the responsibilities are shared or allocated. Other areas of academic librarian responsibilities—such as department liaison, supervision of students and staff, research and publication—might indirectly make use of Extra-Help Librarians to gather information in different phases of a project or related activities. Basically, is incidental and it may also depend on a supervisor's confidence in the Extra-Help Librarian's abilities. Other potential tasks:

- Class assignment assistance
- Orientation tours
- Collaborate in subject tutorials and guides

REFERENCE & INSTRUCTION

Academic librarians are involved in many projects that offer accessible information to students and faculty. Covering reference and instruction areas, librarians maintain in-person contacts, as well as design and produce instructional materials. Extra-Help Librarians are involved in various ways that depend on the needs of an area or a project and even on the full delegation of an activity.

Even though reference and instruction are sometimes separated, responsibilities can intertwine. Just for organization purpose, they will be discussed separately to make it easier to understand the duties that can be delineated to each area. Also, this distinction guide Extra-Help Librarians to a better viewpoint of the library and of potential duties.

REFERENCE

Historically, reference has been a focal point in librarians work, combining subject knowledge and interpersonal skills to serve the clientele. Incremental changes introduced to libraries, especially technological, have been modifying reference services. The reduction of reference materials in print to expanding online resources, the shift from desk reference to roving librarians and even changes in signage from reference desk to information desk indicates an overall adjustment of reference services. Therefore, Extra-Help Librarians' familiarity with changes in the workplace and resources are of key importance to assess their role and their value.

The size of the institution can affect collection organization as far as volume and location, spreading it over various floors and even buildings. Many areas of study, possibly located in different buildings in the same campus, often have their own library and collections. For instance, media viewing and production areas occupy space depending on the departments that it supports, such as liberal arts courses in drama or theater, film production and applied technology. Considering multiple scenarios, Extra-Help Librarians might cover a variety of study areas and library locations. In smaller institutions, offering fewer programs, responsibilities generally include cross-departmental assignments, supporting reference, technical services and instruction. Obviously more in-depth professional knowledge is required when temporarily replacing specialist librarians. Therefore, experience in the field or added training is necessary. In situations that allow for planning in advance, such as sabbatical or maternity leave, training can narrow gaps. Overall, knowing or learning about patrons' specific needs in each location boosts confidence and improves performance. Particularly in reference there are many resources in print and online that are necessary tools to fulfill patrons' information needs, some of which are listed in the next page.

- Basic reference materials
- Specialized periodicals
- Citation style manuals
- General and subject databases
- Subject textbooks in reserve
- Statistical sources
- Subscription and Open Access Journals
- Other Resources

The size of the university and courses offered determine library resource availability. Small campuses with one library covering various fields of study, or a research university with several specialty libraries, manage resources differently. But both make decisions based largely on the types and formats of academic programs offered. Consequently, when librarians consider databases for selection, they often mix some that cover various educational fields and others that are very specialized, prioritizing those that are more in line with their patrons' needs.

Electronic access to library materials from anywhere and anytime has radically changed reference. But it also has accelerated changes in collection management, leading to the decline of print sources, especially of specialized journals. It is noticeable that, even though on-campus and long distance students have different usage patterns, student needs to access library resources online have in general influenced acquisition decisions. Availability and accessibility are essential elements that affect usage and format preferences. Also, Extra-Help Librarians awareness of accessibility rights for library services provided to faculty and students is important to inform them about the following services:

- Interlibrary loans
- Borrowing privileges, fines and fees, renewals and recalls
- Reserves of print, multimedia and e-reserve materials
- Off-campus access to online resources
- Student's assignments and research consultations with librarians
- Librarian Liaison appointments
- Photocopies based on copyright laws

Decreasing print collections and assignment deadlines makes the reference interview even more important to accurately assess students' needs in order to refer them to the best research resources. Also, interaction among students, faculty and librarians requires substantial efforts to reach effective outcomes. Open communications between faculty and librarians about upcoming assignments are crucial. For example, faculty requests of materials and suggestions, assignment deadlines and other relevant details are important departmental information. When Extra-Help Librarians are not directly involved in cooperative decisions between librarians and faculty, regular updates are of a high priority to maintain reference quality to students.

Information & Learning Commons

Even though the differentiation of information and learning commons is in progress (Wolf at al., 2010), the concept revolves around collaboration and communication. Space structures differ, but they often include writing centers, computer labs and reference librarian access. This combines various professional skills to promote students' study abilities to research, organize and present effectively. Extra-Help Librarians guide students to these areas to receive more assistance. They might also be involved in parts of activities at the computer lab and even in technology workshops. Specific tasks are defined by the type of hands-on responsibilities assigned to them. Therefore, it is an area to learn how they are structured and staffed, as well as software availability and usability. Most computer labs would have word processing, spreadsheet, graphics and animation software available. Librarians' responsibilities in this area are still evolving.

INSTRUCTION

Library Instruction is increasingly becoming an essential part of a librarian's work in academic libraries. Inclusion of information literacy in the curriculum varies widely amongst institutions, but the level of librarian skills and the knowledge required or desired encompasses at least some of these basic elements:

- Teaching and research abilities
- Organizational skills and multi-tasking abilities
- Instruction strategies and design
- Knowledge of learning technologies
- Familiarity with Information Literacy Standards
- Curriculum knowledge
- Assessment of students and library services
- Collaboration/ team work qualities
- Knowledge of print and electronic resources
- Presentation skills
- Technology competence

Academic librarians tend to have interest in specific fields, such as science or art, and some engage in research and publishing. However, Extra-Help Librarians in such environment are not under the expectation to produce articles, reviews, books or other items. In reality, their situation can be challenging because acceptance into the Extra-Help Librarians pool does not translate into immediate or regular work. It is not uncommon to be in the pool and not get any assignment, sparse work and limited teaching of a class or two per semester.

Information Literacy

Generally speaking, there is no uniformity on the type and duration of the information literacy instruction implemented in academic libraries. Practices vary in each institution, especially in regard to administration support of library instruction initiatives and the establishment of requirements for students to attend classes in library literacy skills. Faculty recognition of the benefits of such classes, and their willingness to collaborate with librarians, are essential steps to successful programs.

Library resources are often introduced during student orientation, lectures in the library, classrooms, workshops and courses. Self-paced, or under a librarian's instruction, literacy skills are acquired attending classes in-person, online or a combination of both. Courses are generally electives, lasting over a semester or just a one time 30 to 50 minute session. They might be required for freshman or anytime before graduation. Some colleges do not provide formal literacy information to students. Institutions that make them available offer them in different formats, as follow:

- Credit (1 or 3 credits)
- Non-credit
- Embedded in student's online classes

Instruction guidelines are based on the five ACRL's Information Literacy Competency Standards for Higher Education (Neely, 2006). Librarians use these standards as benchmarks to assess students' information literacy, as stated at http://www.ala.org/acrl/standards/informationliteracycompetency, enabling them to:

- *Determine the extent of information needed*
- *Access the needed information effectively and efficiently*
- *Evaluate information and its sources critically*
- *Incorporate selected information into one's knowledge base*
- *Use information effectively to accomplish a specific purpose*
- *Understand the economic, legal, and social issues surrounding the use of information, and access and use information ethically and legally*

Information Literacy assessment tools and resources are available in abundance (Blevens, 2012), supporting the evaluation of students. The following are examples of tests and organization that are focused on developing or providing information to librarians seeking to produce a measurement of literacy outcomes:

- iSkills
  http://www.ets.org/iskills/
- Project SAILS (Standardized Assessment of Information Literacy Skills).
  https://www.projectsails.org/

- Bay Area Community Colleges Information Competency Assessment Project
  http://www.topsy.org/ICAP/ICAProject.html
- National Institute for Learning Outcomes Assessment Organization (NILOA)
  http://learningoutcomeassessment.org/
- Internet Resources for Higher Education Outcomes Assessment
  http://www2.acs.ncsu.edu/UPA/assmt/resource.htm

As far as content, the length of orientations, lectures or courses limits the subjects taught. Topics will certainly be shaped differently for each group of parents, students and faculty with focus on relevant facts and resources, staff interest and availability and the importance of participation. Librarian instructors prioritize aspects that are considered crucial to students' research abilities. Therefore, much emphasis is given to the following:

- Website access
- Library hours for the semester
- Online and print resources available
- 24/7 services
- Computer Lab–hours and equipment
- Research process and skills
- Specific subject area database information
- Citation styles and rules
- Plagiarism, copyright and intellectual property issues
- Source analysis and critical thinking approaches
- Lectures, workshops schedules
- Invisible web

Library instruction aims to work with the faculty to set specific research strategies that provide students with the needed tools to become independent thinkers and evaluators. Students' clear grasp of the research process is invaluable to academic achievement and as professionals in the marketplace. Extra-Help Librarians with reference and or teaching responsibilities have to be able to communicate effectively in face-to-face and online environments, support and engage students and manage technology challenges.

Instruction & Technology

Library instruction is actively adapting the use of technology into lectures and the classroom. Initially there is a sharp learning curve but it proves worthwhile. The incorporation of various tools is transforming how content is presented, changing the interaction between librarian instructors and students. Libraries are at various phases of advancement, but as they identify needs, learn about options and advantages and allocate funds to these initiatives more libraries delve into current instruction trends. These considerations vary depending on the type of learning environment: class attendance on-campus, online classes or a combination of both. The emphasis that institutions put into E-learning also plays a role. For instance, the use of technology has facilitated an increase in long distance classes. Librarians also take advantage of this and promote their own classes, such as Research Skills and Methods.

Extra-Help Librarians that have instruction responsibility or are supporting literacy instructors and researchers are affected by any changes or upgrades. As do other librarians, they also need to pursue digital literacy themselves to continue to provide students and faculty with the information they need through up-and-coming technology. The evaluation of tools available and comparability issues are crucial to any venture into the realm of software use. Some tools have become standard already. Others are still in experimentation. Samples of the many tools librarians are already using, or are considering to utilize in their workplace, are presented from hereon.

Course/Learning Management System (CMS/LMS)

Universities and colleges choose the systems that seem most adequate to their needs and means. CMS features make it possible for instructors and students to provide and access content. It is used as the channel of communication for online courses' face-to-face interaction, as a depository for a syllabus, for assignment submissions and for evaluation tools. There are combinations of other features as well. Librarians' knowledge of their institutions' CMS are able to diversify library outreach. They make content available to students and also to faculty using various strategies, such as embedding resources in departmental courses. Library and faculty collaboration makes it possible to insert essential library information into courses, such as library contact, links to databases, LibGuides and videos. Through the Course Management Systems, students attending classes on and off campus have this flexible option to access library resources via their courses. CMS also give librarian instructors the ability to offer library courses, such as Information Literacy, Research Methods, and others, as another way to inform students and make resources available online. Examples of CMS in use are:

- Blackboard/Angel/WebCT   www.blackboard.com
- eCollege   http://www.ecollege.com/
- Moodle   http://moodle.org/

Classroom Management Systems

Workshops, lectures, and even short informational sessions to students often require librarians to manage the classroom. Usage of systems that give the instructor a view of students' computer screens and the content they are focused on can facilitate the learning process. They are especially helpful when teaching a large number of students and also when there is an indication of misbehavior. Besides supervising screens systems allow chatting, pushing files, quizzes to students and more. Systems currently available are included in the list ahead.

- NetSupport http://www.netsupport-inc.com/
- Apple Remote Desktop v.3 http://www.apple.com/remotedesktop/
- ClassSpot http://tidebreak.com/products/classspot
- iTALC http://italc.sourceforge.net/
- KnowledgeWEB Systems http://www.comweb.com/products/kws_01.htm
- LanSchool v7.4 http://www.lanschool.com/lanschool
- LINK Systems http://www.acs-linksystems.com/
- NetOp School 5.0 http://www.fyxm.net/
- Sanako Study 500 http://www.sanako.com/en-gb/products/study-500/
- SMART Sync http://smarttech.com/sync

Tracking Statistics & Feedback

The implementation of tracking statistics software is an efficient way to obtain quantitative data about the usage of resources. Reliable information is stored and accessible, allowing the identification of patterns. Utilization of the data helps to improve areas that are not reaching the targeted audience. For instance, these methods give an overview of students' engagements at various points of a course:

- DeskTracker http://www.desktracker.com/
- LibAnalytics http://www.springshare.com/libanalytics/
- Clickers http://www.iclicker.com/

Citation Management

A plethora of materials in different formats—including books, databases, websites, e-books and blogs—added to the various citation styles rules, makes citation management tools very desirable. They track research paper resources, add footnotes and create reference lists and bibliographies. Each one of them offers ways to facilitate the organization of tasks that used to be considered difficult by researchers and students. Citations are made easier, even though it takes practice and attention to comparability issues with other tools to achieve the expected results. There are various providers of citation organization and some are listed below.

- CitationMachine http://citationmachine.net/index2.php
- CiteULike http://www.citeulike.org/
- EndNotes http://endnote.com/
- KnightCite http://www.calvin.edu/library/knightcite/
- Mendeley http://www.mendeley.com/
- Qiqqa http://www.qiqqa.com/
- RefWorks http://www.refworks.com/
- Zotero http://www.zotero.org/
- Write-N-Cite http://www.refworks-cos.com/refworks/Write-n-Cite/

―― Plagiarism Detectors

Increased access to World Wide Web resources, as well as copy and paste capabilities, facilitates plagiarism. The development of free and commercial software has improved the identification of copying and unauthorized content usage. It is critical to make students aware of the misuse of information. Therefore, librarians make efforts to teach, through lectures and courses, the concepts of ethics, copyright laws, as well as paraphrasing and summarizing techniques. Plagiarism detectors are used not to punish students, but to raise consciousness about their actions and the damage they promote to others. Examples of this type of software include:

- Academic Plagiarism   http://www.academicplagiarism.com/
- Chimpsky   http://chimpsky.uwaterloo.ca/
- Copyscape   http://www.copyscape.com/
- Ithenticate   http://www.ithenticate.com/
- Plagiarism Detect   http://www.plagiarismdetect.com/
- Plagium   http://www.plagium.com/
- PlagScan   http://www.plagscan.com/
- Turnitin   http://turnitin.com/en_us/home
- SafeAssign   http://help.blackboard.com/student/content/ _safeassign/safeassign_about.htm

―― Conferencing & Presentation Tools

Free and fee-based conferencing and presentation tools are frequently complimentary. Librarians utilize them in virtual reference, instruction and outreach. One of the main advantages of conferencing tools is that they permit the connection of a number of people in one session. Free services allow fewer people to connect at the same time and subscription based services offer the advantage of connecting more people. Presentation tools help lecturers and trainers condense content and enhance participants' experience, especially for visual learners. Through course management systems or other online services, content is shared, allowing demonstration of resources such as databases and websites. Here are some of the tools available in the marketplace:

- Interactive Whiteboards & Smartboards Eno   http://www.polyvision.com/
- SMART Boards   http://smarttech.com/smartboard
- ooVoo   http://www.oovoo.com/home.aspx
- PowerPoint   http://office.microsoft.com/en-us/powerpoint/
- Prezi   http://prezi.com/
- Skype   http://www.skype.com/intl/en-us/features/
- StarBoard   http://us.hitachisolutions.com/starboard/products/ StarBoard_Software.shtml
- Adobe Connect   http://www.adobe.com/ap/products/adobeconnect.html

- Blackboard Collaborate (Elluminate/Wimba)
  http://www.blackboard.com/Platforms/Collaborate/Products/Blackboard-Collaborate.aspx
- WebEx   http://www.webex.com/webinars/How-to-share-a-presentation

Content Creation & Sharing

Collaboration among faculty, students, librarians and even the administration is made possible using tools to create and share documents, including videos, images and links. Account authentication for access to make additions, save and archive (Kroski, 2009) is a necessary step to maintain accountability and quality. Service providers can offer content creators a range of features in which to make needed adjustments. Examples of such providers are:

- Connexions   http://cnx.org/
- Dropbox   https://www.dropbox.com/features
- Googledocs   http://www.google.com/google-d-s/b1.html
- Lecshare   http://lecshare.com/index.htm
- LibGuides   http://springshare.com/libguides/
- PBWorks   http://pbworks.com/education
- SharePoint   http://sharepoint.microsoft.com/en-us/Pages/default.aspx
- SoftChalk   http://softchalk.com/

Content Editing Software

Instruction materials for presentation, posted online or reproduced in print, can be done more easily by the use of content editing tools with set features to improve layout and visual impact. Libraries and other educational environments utilize the software below in their materials production process.

- Camtasia; Snagit; Jing; Screencast   http://www.techsmith.com
- Captivate   http://www.adobe.com/products/captivate.html

Audio & Video Creation

The usage of audio and video in tutorials and presentations, for example, is a dynamic form to present information and demonstrate the steps of a process. It also has the potential to reach broader audiences and different learning styles. Free products are available and it is possible to use them without downloading. Besides, the equipment required, such as microphones and cameras with web capabilities, is often inexpensive. Examples of software used by librarians include:

- Screen Toaster
  http://www.makeuseof.com/dir/screentoaster-free-web-based-screen-recording-tool/
- Screen   http://www.screenr.com/
- Screencast-O-Matic   http://www.screencast-o-matic.com/
- CamStudio   http://camstudio.org/

—— Video Hosting & Sharing

Selection of the most suitable video hosting and sharing channels considers audience, material content, ease of use, popularity, cost and other things. Decrease in the cost of technology devices, especially mobile versions, and an increase in students' use of these innovations, have been strong incentives for libraries to disseminate information through videos, webcasts, podcasts and in other ways. Once uploaded to the selected channel(s) the information is accessible from anywhere at anytime. The following spaces, among many others, are often used:

- Colleges and universities websites
- YouTube   http://www.youtube.com/
- Vimeo   http://vimeo.com/
- Vzaar   http://vzaar.com/

—— Survey Creation & Assessment

Feedback is of great importance to evaluate the efficacy of strategies used by the instructor and to determine the level of knowledge acquired by the students. Therefore, the types of survey questions, applications, features, frequency of use and data analyses are a few of the aspects to consider when comparing the options. There is a variety of survey creation software available and some offer free simplified versions. A sample of them is listed for further consideration:

- Google Forms   http://www.google.com/google-d-s/forms/
- iSkills   http://www.ets.org/iskills/about
- Poll Everywhere   http://www.polleverywhere.com/
- SurveyMonkey   http://www.surveymonkey.com/
- Sails   https://www.projectsails.org/
- Techneos   http://www.techneos.com/

—— E-Portfolio

A multimedia organization tool used for many purposes, e-portfolios offers the ability to create, gather, select and display materials based most likely on relevance. It also allows addition of files, documents or images, to showcase individuals' work in a class, program or career. Librarians use e-portfolio in different scenarios. They can use it personally to record their career growth, in instruction to share information and to support students' e-portfolios. Consideration of hardware and software, support and ownership, safety and privacy, access and maintenance (Lorenzo, 2005) are some elements to considering when creating e-portfolios. Examples of such platforms are listed in the following page.

- e-Portfolio   http://www.eportfolio.org/
- Digication   http://www.digication.com/
- Foliotek   http://www.foliotek.com/
- Mahara   https://mahara.org/
- RCampus   http://www.rcampus.com/
- Desire2Learn   http://www.desire2learn.com/products/learning-suite/

QR–Quick Response Code

Mobile devices have launched new ways of connecting from anywhere, anytime and quick response code is designed to "link physical spaces with mobile-friendly web resources" (van Armhem, 2012), making it easier to access places and information already created with other tools. Libraries can encode website addresses, links to Ask-a-Librarian, phone numbers, library bookshelves and other resources that can fulfill library patrons' needs and engage them in the process. Users of QR codes need a camera and web connection capability in their mobile device to access the information made available by libraries and other organizations. Examples of companies that offer QR code creators and readers (Byrne, 2011) are shown below:

QR code creators

- QR Droid   http://www.qrdroid.com/generate
- Azon Media   http://www.azonmedia.com/qrcode-generator
- Delivr   http://www.delivr.com/qr-code-generator

QR code readers

- BeeTagg   http://www.beetagg.com/en/
- i-nigma Reader   http://www.i-nigma.com/i-nigmahp.html
- QuickMark   http://www.quickmark.cn/En/basic/index.asp
- ScanLife   http://www.scanlife.com/en/

In sum, technology advancements have impacted education in general and long distance education in particular. Academic institutions offer a variety of programs and services to support students' achievements on-campus and through distance environments. As demonstrated in the library environment, there is an ever increasing number of tools requiring investment in software, hardware and training to implement new learning strategies. Access 24/7 and continuing development of newer and better digital sources and formats require innovative approaches.

In this new context, librarians have an active role in rethinking how to present the resources and services available to reach the patrons, faculty and students in particular. In addition to collaborating with faculty, librarians actively acquire databases, create LibGuides, offer literacy courses, embed library information in faculty's courses and make reference available through chat or Ask-a-Librarian and other initiatives.

Extra-Help Librarians can be involved in many hands-on projects such as compiling bibliographic references, tutorials, responding to chat interactions and teaching literacy and research skills courses. Performance in digital environments requires knowledge of web technologies and applications to design materials and to involve students. Therefore, professional experience and a level of engagement can effect the types of assignments they are involved in. There are challenges in terms of task delegation, training and funds. But reference and instruction have been evolving and opportunities for Extra-Help Librarians are bound to expand as well.

---— CHAPTER REFERENCES ——---

ACRL Research Planning and Review Committee (2010). 2010 top ten trends in academic libraries: A review of the current literature. *College & Research Libraries News,* Jun, 71, 6, Jun, 286-292.

Blevens, C. (2012) Catching up with information literacy assessment. Resources for program evaluation. *College & Research Libraries News,* 73, 4, Apr, 202-206.

Byrne, R. (2011). QR codes go to school. *School Library Journal*, 57, 12, Dec, 16.

Hisle, L. (2002). *Higher education funding. C&RL News,* 63, 10, Nov.

Kroski, E. (2009). That's infotainment! *School Library Journal*, 55, 2, Feb, 40-42.

Lorenzo, G., & Ittelson, J. (2005). *An overview of e-portfolio.* D. Oblinger (Ed.). *EDUCASE.* Retrieved from http://net.educause.edu/ir/library/pdf/ELI3001.pdf

Neely, T. (Ed.). (2011). *How to stay afloat in the academic library job pool*. Chicago, IL: ALA.

Neely, T. (2006). *Information Literacy Assessment: standards-based tools and assignments.* Chicago, IL: ALA.

Van Arnhem, J. & Burton, C. (2012). QR Codes: what's the payoff? *The Charleston Advisor,* Jan, 13, 3, 56-57.

Wolf, J., Neylor, T, & Drueke, J. (2010). The role of the academic reference librarian in the learning commons. *Reference & User Services Quarterly, 50, 2, Winter, 108-113.*

SCHOOL LIBRARIES 5

School districts goals are to provide a high level of education even with minimum resources. Noticeably, the pressure on them increases as funds are cut and priorities are reviewed. Such conditions impact school libraries heavily. They are losing funds allocated to maintain librarian jobs and collections. However, efforts continue to be centered on providing the expected level of service to their community. Even though permanent school librarians are struggling to keep their jobs, support staff is still needed, even if occasionally. Therefore, it is relevant to introduce the role of Extra-Help Librarians in this setting. Even in critical situations they continue to be a library's staff option. As libraries get more financial support, assignment frequencies are likely to increase. Most importantly, the focus is on professional development and the training of future librarians in the pursuit of careers in school libraries.

School librarians have many responsibilities, but they focus primarily on supporting the curriculum, in teaching and in engaging students to learn to read and develop their research skills. To reach such goals librarians acquire collection materials and plan activities. Librarians normally work solo, perhaps with the assistance of circulation clerks and volunteers, depending on the school's size and the availability of funds.

Extra-Help Librarians working in an environment without another librarian's direct supervision will require self-discipline, knowledge and confidence to perform well. They interact with students of various ages and grade levels, have knowledge of the curriculum, search the catalog and online resources and perform basic administrative tasks. District level support might be available for technology problems, but daily duties need to be effectively handled locally. Factors of this nature weigh on how well Extra-Help Librarians adapt to the school environment and on their general success.

Organization

Public or private schools are organized in a variety of grade level combinations, from elementary school up to high school. Elementary schools include pre-school, kindergarten alone or combined with other leves, lower grade school, and even Middle school/Junior High. High School are usually separated from the others. Like other organizations, the size and model of the school impacts personnel needs. Staff layers influence the levels of autonomy of each job category. School organizations normally vary from institution to institution, but the following layers are often present in their structures:

> School District Superintendent School Media Specialist
> School Principal Teachers
> School Boards Administrative Staff
> Media Specialist District Supervisor Friends of the Library
> Extra-Help Librarians and Teachers Volunteers

Extra-Help Librarians are more likely to be placed at the school district level, unless a single school has autonomy and needs to set their own pool. In general, single schools handle long term absences with volunteers or even opt to close the library temporarily.

JOB TITLES

Librarians in school settings have acquired several different job titles over the years because their roles have evolved. Factors such as the size of the school district or school, students grade levels, technology use and supervision duties have influenced titles choices. Some examples are illustrated by:

- School districts are large enough a librarian oversees other school libraries and/or supervises other librarians, librarian aids and volunteers.
- School educational levels, elementary or high school, require librarians to use different strategies to guide students through the learning process.
- Librarians using technology as a teaching tool to promote resources and monitor students learning in the library media center.

Therefore, librarians' responsibilities often generate preferences for specific titles as listed below:

> School Librarian
> School Media Specialist
> School Media Coordinator
> School Media Center Librarian

Librarian Media Specialist
Teacher Librarian

The American Association of School Librarians (AASL) recognizes that the broader title of School Librarian is a more uniform job title for librarians working in schools. However, the increasing incorporation of technology and instruction in the librarian roles at schools has added new dimensions to the title.

PROFESSIONAL CREDENTIALS & QUALIFICATIONS

School librarians need to be certified teachers and study specific library issues in this area through an ALA certified institution. The reverse case is also common, where librarians need to obtain teacher's certification to fulfill Librarian Teacher positions requirements. Not all schools require the applicant to hold both certifications, but it is certainly an advantage to have them. Additional information is available through Library Schools and the State Department of Education.

TEACHER CERTIFICATION

The State Board of Education or the Certification Advisory Committee regulates teachers certification. It can be obtained for elementary grades or for one or more subjects. Verify with the appropriate institution about the requirements to get the certification, since they vary by state. For example, California (http://www.ctc.ca.gov/credentials/teach.html) requires separate credentials to teach different grade levels or special education. Teachers need to earn the Multiple Subject Teaching Credential to work in elementary schools, the Single Subject Teaching Credential for high schools and an Education Specialist Instruction Credential to teach special education students. The state of New York offers many types of teacher certificates and there is one even for teacher substitutes which has its own requirements (http://www.highered.nysed.gov/tcert/certificate/substituteteaching.html). These examples show that there is a need to understand the relevant teaching credentialing process to evaluate the feasibility of working in school libraries. This is particularly true either for short-term jobs as Extra-Help Librarian or future career goals as a permanent school librarian.

LIBRARY MEDIA SPECIALIST CERTIFICATION

ALA accredited schools offering MLIS degrees generally present students with choices of programs dedicated to various types of libraries, including Teacher Librarianship. In this track, courses are focused on school library issues which give students without a teaching background a more in depth overview of the field. It is necessary to obtain a teacher credential from a State's Commission on Teacher Credentialing.

The need to acquire the two credentials is explained in the MLIS and Teacher Librarianship Student Handbook available at the San Jose State University website, http://slisweb.sjsu.edu/classes/tlmlis/tlmlis_toc.htm.

NATIONAL BOARD CERTIFIED LIBRARY MEDIA SPECIALIST

Librarian certification by the National Board for Professional Teaching Standards (NBPTS) (http://www.nbpts.org/) is not a requirement to work in a library school. But it is a considerable step in professional development, providing personal and professional gains. Librarians interested in furthering their education to reach higher intellectual goals, professional recognition and financial rewards may consider this certificate as a path to potential opportunities to achieve them.

GENERAL QUALIFICATIONS

Schools usually have a library, are assisted by a district library, have classroom libraries or a combination of some or all of these. Therefore, the library materials organization level can be widespread, from basic literary books and textbooks on teachers' classrooms to being located in high technology libraries. Consequently, school librarians' professional requirements involve:

- Teaching license and school librarian credential
- Familiarity with school curriculum
- Knowledge of children's and young adult literature
- Understanding of current trends in library media services
- Computer experience in library media
- Instruction and research skills
- Administrative and supervisory skills

Extra-Help Librarians also need these specialized skills to work at school libraries. Their quick adaptation to the school community and daily routines as well as the ability to handle computer problems or children's misbehavior can be advantageous in a school environment.

PRACTICAL & THEORETICAL ISSUES

Schools are diverse environments making them susceptible to controversies. Many issues of practical and theoretical content arise and school librarians have to manage them because of the effects that they have on their work. Some examples mentioned here are related to administrative, legal and educational matters. Issues of critical importance, such as No Child Left Behind (NCLB), States Testing Standard, copyright and internet access laws, generate demands on school libraries and librarian's performance. Issues of a more generic nature that school librarians confront include:

- Policies and procedures
- Open and restricted shelves
- Reading and visualization strategies
- Student diversity
- English Language Learners (ELL)
- Teaching and learning styles
- Subject standards by grade level
- Homework help
- Quantifiable student achievement
- Literacy initiatives and focus
- Technology use to support curriculum
- Assistive technology and curriculum standards
- Fundraising

Librarian Responsibilities

GENERAL & SPECIFIC AREAS

General librarian responsibilities encompass various areas and some of them are categorized below to provide an overview of librarians coordination needs:

- Develop collection to support curriculum
- Co-teach as necessary
- Program design and implementation
- Engage in reading mediation with children, parents, teachers and other staff
- Network internally and externally
- Share information with staff and administration

These responsibilities unfold on to other more specific duties. Therefore, more details are presented below to facilitate the understanding of the activities that school librarians are involved with. Also, it gives Extra-Help a quick guide in identifying aspects of the absent librarian's routine, allowing them to continue it either on a short or long term basis. Four areas are delineated in the next page.

1 — Administrative duties

- Read materials reviews
- Select, acquire, catalog, process, display, maintain and weed materials
- Collection inventory
- Track book donation (local bookstores, Amazon.com accounts)
- Schedule class instruction and visits, events, and meetings
- Reserve computer for group sessions
- Display students' class projects
- Update reading lists
- Work on bibliographies by subject
- Maintain reading logs
- Review and update tutors list
- Program events
- Keep records
- Budget
- Collect data and write reports
- Volunteers recruitment, training and supervision
- Participate in the Friends of the Library meetings
- Research and write grants
- Maintain library website pages and links
- Technology troubleshooting
- Keep log of computer repairs
- Oversee circulation
- Issue overdue notices
- Participate in staff meetings
- Create and maintain the Extra-Help Librarians Handbook

2— Student instruction, monitoring and supervision

- New student orientation
- Familiarization with Dewey Decimal Classification System
- Research guidance
- Promote safety: physical and psychological
- Foster creativity: verbal and written
- Generate reading enthusiasm
- Reading levels information
- Reluctant and accelerated readers
- Storytime by grade/class

- Reading buddies programs
- Behavioral conflict resolution
- Homework help
- Extended accessibility before and after school

3 — Librarian and teacher collaboration

- Curriculum co-planning
- Co-teach various ages and grades
- Bibliography development
- Suggestions and requests of library materials
- Procedures for class time at the library
- Define information literacy instruction goals
- Establish instructional delivery formats
- On-going or periodic reading and/or writing assessment
- Participate in teachers meetings
- New teachers library orientation
- Teachers collection

4 — Events Management & Participation

- Parents' orientation tours
- Parent and teacher conferences
- Children's Book Week
- Banned Books Week
- Holidays - events /displays
- Year/semester ending activities

SPECIAL EVENTS

The curriculum is a source of vast learning opportunities and school librarians initiate or support classroom initiatives to engage students. Some events take considerable planning, requiring much effort before, during and after. The extent and complexity of the work Extra-Help Librarians have depend on variables such as assignment length and how far along the planning of the event has reached. In general, Extra-Help have limited chances to participate in special events, unless they are working in long-term assignments. In such a case, embracing responsibilities for the event can still happen even in the absence of the permanent librarian. Following are some significant examples of such events.

AUTHORS & SPEAKER VISITS

When authors or speakers are scheduled to visit a school, librarian and teachers have opportunities to coordinate activities around the event. Planning can involve extensive preparation and a variety of students' projects. Students can use the library's print and online resources to gather information about the author to create related projects. Research, reading and writing can develop through some of the activities below:

- Read author's books
- Locate author's website
- Biography search
- Author interview
- Book signing requests
- Writing workshops
- Visit evaluation
- Thank you notes to author

Another option that some schools take advantage of is the virtual author visit. This is a more cost effective way that schools have to give students an opportunity to learn about an author and his or her work. Through in-person or virtual author contacts, students can learn the importance of reading and writing.

BOOK FAIR

Promoting book fairs can help school libraries get revenues to invest in materials, to further generate donations and build community. Many libraries depend on book fairs to supplement materials budgets; especially with dwindling contributions from other funding sources, in particular the state. Librarian and teachers take the opportunity to release a list of desired books. Children and their relatives' donations to the library and classrooms contribute to improve the collection. As an incentive, libraries create bookplates for donor recognition. Also, there might be simultaneous programs happening. Some of the options involve:

- Book character appearances
- Family dinner fundraisers
- Weekend breakfasts
- Book talks
- Movie shows

Publishing companies such as Scholastic (http://www.scholastic.com/bookfairs/) and Usborne Books (http://www.usbornebooks.com/usborne-book-fairs.html) offer school libraries opportunities and incentives to promote book fairs. They offer discounts, marketing materials, vendor support, and other possibilities. Volunteers can be an important factor to make this event viable. Their contribution in setting-up, staffing and putting away books and other materials is crucial. Also, volunteers help with other librarian strategies to engage participation and attract working parents in the evenings and weekend, such as providing optional childcare.

OPEN HOUSE & BACK TO SCHOOL NIGHT

In occasions like an open house or back to school, the library showcases their collection and mount displays of library materials and students' works. They provide an opportunity to welcome parents accompanying their child or browsing on their own. Competition with class time can detract parents, guardians and relatives from visiting the library, but it can still raise library awareness. In addition, it can provide an opportunity to recruit volunteers and even receive donations. Presentation is important in terms of the organization of the space, as well as staff and volunteer friendliness.

COLLECTION ORGANIZATION

School districts often combine schools, such as middle schools and secondary schools, in the same building complex or somewhat near each other. Consequently, the differences might not be as obvious as when these schools are housed separately and in different locations. Such considerations are important for libraries due to space and collections. In a K-6 school, the collection focuses more on picture books, fairy tales, easy readers and chapter books and informational books. The language level is appropriate for the lower grades. They are also placed on shorter, lower shelves to be more accessible to children's exploration and usage. The space is more nurturing in the lower grades, while at the Junior High and High School level library space becomes more task-oriented. In upper grades, space is utilized to accommodate the collection as well as to provide students with room for study groups and independent study, computer labs and media. Extra-Help Librarians' familiarity with such differences will help them adapt more quickly, assisting the school community with less disturbance.

Even though computers are increasing in numbers and usage, but books are still a predominant format in school libraries. High interest books, and other titles that are required for reading assignments, are included in the collection. To make collection items easy to find they are organized by type and format. Non-fiction materials in most school libraries are organized following the Dewey Decimal Classification System.

Other ways used to better identify materials is to subdivide or label books by historical, realistic, fantasy, accelerated reading or by literary award winners such as Caldecott and Newbery. Sections and codes are often similar to public libraries, see Table No. 3.1. The uniqueness of each school library and the librarian expertise can also play a part in the organization of materials. The fact that schools serve determined age groups and have a somewhat limited collection allows more flexibility in its organization and display.

High School libraries or Media Centers provide additional information, placing hand-outs, booklets and flyers in special sections or displays, in the following interest areas:

- Different types of majors
- College scholarships programs
- List of colleges and universities
- Placement tests (SAT, foreign language)
- College financial aid
- College catalogs
- Reading and writing assessments

COLLECTION & SERVICES

A library's amount of non-English materials depends on the school demographics and the languages offered by the curriculum. Materials to serve children with bilingual needs are acquired to support the development of children's English skills. Besides providing materials to serve students that speak other languages than English, there are staff professionals that benefit from such a collection. Among them are specialists in children language development, bilingual teachers and aids and parents who might need such materials themselves. Junior High and High School curriculum offer foreign languages, such as Spanish and French, and the library can provide supplementary materials. The input of the teacher of such languages should be instrumental in the library's ordering process.

Referrals to other libraries or literacy programs are used to cover areas that the school library collection or services might not be able to provide. Outside resources are often necessary since school libraries have limited space and funds. Reaching out to other institutions also demonstrate the school's commitment to serving its community.

STAFF COLLECTION

Resources are also available to staff, professional and leisure items. The usage of current materials, suggestions and feedback contributes to development and improvement of this collection. Counselors, nurses, speech therapists and other staff suggest materials for purchase in their area of expertise. Books, journals and databases can fulfill staff needs that could be more difficult to meet individually. Librarians support such collections to provide a service to other professionals at the school and to develop collaboration. Informed Extra-Help Librarians know about its' location and the checkout procedures to correctly maintain staff accounts.

ACQUISITION, INVENTORY & WEEDING

Annual inventory serves to analyze various aspects of the collection. It provides a picture of the items on hand, not yet returned and missing. It identifies subject gaps and weeding needs which may result in future acquisition plans. School library collections aim to keep materials current in accord with curricular changes. Outdated material is discarded and new materials are added based on specific sections of the curriculum, as well as new projects developed by various teachers. Collaboration between teachers and librarians is especially important when considering weeding and the acquisition of materials. This interaction contributes to a more targeted collection, adds different perspectives and potentially leads to an increase in usage and the fulfilling of students' and teachers' needs.

Extra-Help Librarians awareness of these efforts leads to a closer observance of guidelines, the detection of relevant materials and suggestions for additions. Therefore, they show support to the permanent librarian collection maintenance goals.

CIRCULATION SUPPORT

School libraries have very limited financial resources to be able to employ circulation aids. Consequently, the librarian is often also the circulation person when there is not a clerk or volunteer responsible for circulation. Duties include check-in, check-out and tracking of materials as well as shelving whenever necessary. Class volunteers in early grades or library volunteers frequently become assistants. However, the delegation of circulation tasks can be limited because of privacy issues, volunteer short hours and training needs.

Circulation requires continual supervision to keep the collection inventory accurate. In such a contained community, patrons are easily traceable to resolve fines due to late, damaged or lost materials. Parents are held responsible for a student's careless use of materials and resulting fines.

Extra-Help Librarians need to know the circulation rules and procedures well to resolve problems accordingly. Working solo in a school library requires multitasking and prioritization of daily activities. It is a challenge that becomes more manageable over time, in particular when assignments are longer or they are assigned to the same school more often.

Patrons

School libraries go beyond their collections and services. As a community that focuses on children's best interests, it involves several groups of people. Relationships are developed to reach a common goal and the library is an important piece in bringing people and resources together and in supporting and being supported. On a continuous basis the following groups interact:

- Students
- Teachers
- Parents
- Staff

Learning the dynamics and importance of each group is one of the factors that guides Extra-Help Librarians work. Basic information pertinent to each group is presented below.

STUDENTS

Students access the library at various times, such as while waiting for school to start, during lunch break or after school. They can explore the collection or just have a place to be. School libraries have this captive audience and efforts are made to build on their educational growth. Librarians and support staff provide them with an environment where they have opportunities to learn, including the following (Williams, 2009):

- Find good books to read
- Practice skills they learn in class
- Use traditional materials and emerging formats
- Develop new research skills research information they need for assignments
- Learn responsible research practice
- Practice internet safety under guidance
- Apply ethical standards

Strategies to assist students vary considerably depending on the grade levels the library supports, the students' age group, interests and their intellectual strengths and weaknesses. In such a fluid environment, Extra-Help Librarians' knowledge, respect and work ethics are significant elements to best serve students.

BOYS & GIRLS ISSUES

The dynamics among parents, students, teachers, counselors and librarians revolve around the issues that students go through in their academic and social development. Librarians assist students from an early age through adolescence and emerging adulthood. Using their skills and resources, they support students in their gradual transformation. Informed

Extra-Help understand the environment and adapts quickly. It is important that they proceed in accordance with the guidelines of the school when interacting with students, in particular those with difficulties. Below are some of the matters that afflict students, mostly in their adolescence:

- Family relations
- Addictions
- Violence and gangs
- Anorexia
- Depression and suicide
- Body changes
- Discipline and defiance
- Grade expectations and output
  College and career decisions
- School rules
- Relationships
- Teen pregnancy
- Cutting classes
- Sexual orientation
- Introversion
- Control vs. independence

Learning Disabilities

Students' learning difficulties can go undetected, but once identified professional support is usually available at schools. If not, students are referred to other institutions for follow up. School librarians also play a part in such circumstances, developing a collection that contains materials necessary to professional aids, parents and students involved in the process. Librarians often take initiative to increase awareness about the problems. Extra-Help Librarian's familiarity with learning disability programs and a school's strategies to provide students with the needed materials facilitates the management of materials and other informational requests.

Learning disabilities are related to the following health matters:

- ADHD or ADD—Attention-deficit/hyperactivity disorder
- OCD—Obsessive Compulsive Disorder
- Anxiety
- Asperger's
- Depression
- Bipolar
- Fragile X
- Language Disorders
- Dyslexia
- Autism
- Tourette's

A need to understand and cope with any of these issues requires continual monitoring of medical literature. The Child Development Institute (http://www.childdevelopmentinfo.

com/learning/learning_disabilities.shtml) summarizes five general areas affected by learning disabilities:

- Spoken language: delays, disorders, and deviations in listening and speaking
- Written language: difficulties with reading, writing and spelling.
- Arithmetic: difficulty in performing arithmetic operations or in understanding basic concepts
- Reasoning: difficulty in organizing and integrating thoughts
- Memory: difficulty in remembering information and instructions

A vast amount of information about disabilities is available online and in print. The "Assistive and Adaptive Technology Resource" (Cummings, 2011) is an excellent starting list that can be expanded and updated. It is a compilation of organizations' approaches to learning disabilities, speech, hearing and visual impairments, professional development sources and more.

Extra-Help Librarians' familiarity with school or district guidelines on learning disabilities and other sources of support—such as school teachers, psychologists and speech therapists and personal disability students' aids—make them more apt to respond to any inquiries or at least be able to refer students and parents to organizations in their area of need.

READING

Elementary school librarians can provide readers' advice to students and also to parents. Students participate in scheduled class visits to the library for story time and they have the opportunity to browse and choose materials to read. Parents use the library to obtain books and reading suggestions for their children, showing interest in the development of their children's reading skills. This is usually the norm in the lower grades.

In Junior High and in high school students are more in command of their choices. To a degree the curriculum dictates their reading options since they are required to read pre-assigned books. Depending on the class, they have a few alternatives. When there are no requirements or students are reading for pleasure, librarians provide more widespread input. They talk with students about their interests, consider what they need to accomplish and provide suggestions and assistance in the process.

An Extra-Help Librarian's clear understanding of the different needs of lower and upper grade students accelerates their acceptance at a given school's library. Their observation skills and tact are especially valuable in the upper grade schools. Their job assignments are usually too short to develop relationships with students, but it is equally important that they are friendly and at the same time firm and consistent—in particular when enforcing library rules. Knowledge of a curriculum's chosen fiction books and subject areas in non-fiction are a basic way to direct students to pre-assigned books and also a way to provide suggestions.

Readers

The levels of students' motivation to read vary from the uninterested to the avid reader. In either group librarians have opportunities to influence their decisions on fiction and non-fiction materials. Varied strategies are geared to support each of these groups.

Reluctant Readers

Among the issues that librarians are confronted with, it is not unreasonable to say that guiding reluctant readers is challenging and rewarding. Parents and teachers might mention a students' resistance to read, request suggestion and discuss strategies to motivate the student. Otherwise, librarians tend to identify these students through their body language and lack of library involvement. Planning and implementing strategies to attract reluctant readers has been at the center of school libraries' efforts. The acquisition of materials, instruction and the programming of events aim to reach the whole student body. In particular, they try to reach those students that do not show interest in reading. Academic success is highly dependent on reading proficiency and school libraries have a major role in supporting students and teachers to reach these goals. Extra-Help Librarians have to be able to rapidly identify readers' types, their styles and reading preferences to best engage each student group. This can be particularly true regarding those that most need to improve their reading abilities and enjoyment.

Avid Readers

There are administrative difficulties to accommodate avid readers. Since they may read fast, the collection becomes easily exhausted. Interest in a variety of genres available in-house delays the need for referral to other libraries and even in interlibrary loans. At some point these students naturally start seeking other reading sources, such as the public library, and if they have the means they may buy the books they want.

Accelerated Readers Book Lists

Accessible through the library website, in print or even linked to the catalog, accelerated book lists are used for a reader's advisory. These books are grade level specific as a result of reading difficulty and comprehension measurements taken by companies such as Lexile. In a librarian-teacher partnership, a recommendation of Lexile level books are based on discussions about students' needs to follow a structured reading pattern to develop reading confidence and reach other pre-established goals. Extra-Help Librarians familiarity about Lexile measurements, the librarian in charge's usage of accelerated book lists, the location of lists in the library and information whether such lists have been provided to the local public library, all contribute to an efficient service to students and their parents.

BOOKTALK

Librarians "Booktalks" seek to expand students' interests in books and promote readership. Some of the Booktalks may or may not follow curriculum standards. There are Booktalks that are done by the school librarian alone, by a visiting librarian or by combining local and visiting librarians. These usually take class time, most likely English. A variety of books are displayed and briefly described. This can promote discussions, stimulate curiosity and encourage reading.

Extra-Help Librarians who are knowledgeable about appropriate literature for various grades might encounter opportunities to Booktalk. It is advisable to have some favorite books that could be used on short notice. Either way, whenever a reading suggestion is requested or an introduction for a visiting librarian or a Booktalk is needed, the Extra-Help Librarians can take the chance to show their ability to respond promptly.

RESEARCH

School's curriculum standards are set by each State Board of Education (http://www.corestandards.org/in-the-states). Teachers use such guidelines to plan how to best present information to students and reach expected results. Grade level requirements often lead school libraries to invest in the content of the same materials' year after year to maintain consistency. In elementary, middle school and high school librarians develop collections to respond to specific subject area needs. Ancient Civilizations and Periodic Table of the Elements are examples of topics developed into class presentations, arts exhibits and experiments.

Usually such projects demand a variety of research materials. When libraries do not have sufficient materials available for students to do their assignments. As Extra-Help Librarians meet such conditions they should assess the resources in print and online and refer students to other libraries, if necessary. This way they will be able to manage large groups of students doing the same project at the same time more effectively. It is advisable to learn a project's deadline and set strategies to guide students, even when working at a location for one day. Consult the teacher when unclear about the assignments. In an ideal situation, nearby libraries would have been notified of upcoming visit of students searching for books on specific topics. This illustrates that communication between school and public libraries about students' needs facilitates the acquisition and availability of materials to support those needs and school demands. Also, high school relationships with colleges increase emphasis on the development of research abilities, critical thinking and other academic matters.

Extra-Help Librarians ability to adapt to the demands of current class requests and activities in progress makes the transition, for a day or months, easier for staff and students. Handling class visits or a high volume of students in a short period of time can be challenging. Managing to reshelf a great number of books and keep the library orderly and inviting also adds to the pressure. When working solo or supervising other library staff, such practicalities can not be overlooked.

Research Assistance

Technology usage in schools tends to increase from lower to upper grades. Elementary schools are not as centered on the use of computers and other equipments as junior high and high school. Such demands become more considerable as students continue using various types of media in and out of school. Consequently, school librarians have become more media oriented, allocating more time to assist with computers, video and digital cameras and other technologies. Instruction or supervision of students developing projects on various subjects using word processing, PowerPoint and other software, are becoming increasingly more frequent. Librarians also teach how to use the library catalog and about research process basics.

Whenever working at school media centers, Extra-Help Librarians need to be comfortable navigating the library website, using several media tools and have troubleshooting skills to be more productive. Generally the School District buys and maintains the computers and other electronic equipment. Request of the district technical support is often necessary, but knowing how to handle equipment problems may eliminate lengthy waits. Even though contacts with teachers are brief and even sporadic in short assignments, it is an advantage to know how to access a teacher's webpage per subject, their class grades and the class periods. This helps get updates or to anticipate students' research needs to support them in the development of class projects.

Information Literacy

Teaching information literacy to children is developed in school libraries to the extent that the curricular activities and other tasks allow. Even though basic aspects of information literacy are introduced, academic libraries provide a more in depth experience. Examples of common subjects covered:

- School website
- Website domains variations
- Primary and secondary sources
- Databases introduction
- Copyright
- Citation Styles
- Research strategies and source evaluation
- Online safety and social networks

Libraries contribute to students' success at school. To meet expectations they provide a strong collection, programs and activities that develop students' reading, writing and critical thinking skills. In addition, they promote basic information literacy to prepare students to make the transition to college and beyond.

Computer Lab Initiatives

School libraries incorporate computer training and media experimentation mainly in the upper grades. Handling hardware and software, students are motivated to learn word processing, PowerPoint, Excel, web page design and more. Other Media Center initiatives involve:

- Podcasting
- Website building
- Video development
- Newspaper composition
- Yearbook design

Developments in online sharing and collaboration for academic purposes changes teacher/students and student/student learning dynamics. Librarians can intermediate these relationships through the Media Center and integrate chosen systems for use. Discussion of class assignments and difficulties, file sharing, note keeping and features are some options that the following services (Byrne, 2012) offer:

- Google+   https://plus.google.com/
- On Think Binder   http://thinkbinder.com/
- Open Study   http://openstudy.com/
- Study Blue   http://www.studyblue.com/
- Study Hall   http://i1.studyhallapp.com/login.html

PARENTS

Schools in general and school libraries in particular have been distressed with decreasing income and stricter measures to curb expenses. Consequently, a school library's budgeting process prioritizes the criteria (Eberhart, 1991) used to allocate funds, including the following factors:

- Philosophy and goals of the school district
- Intellectual content and level of the collection
- Changes in the curriculum
- Ability levels, learning styles, and social and emotional development of students
- Attrition rate by loss, weeding and ageing of the collection
- Degrees to which the collection includes professional materials for teachers

Considering current allocations for school libraries, parents' involvement has become even more necessary and it has helped guarantee the existence of a number of libraries. Their interest and initiatives are important and some of the ways they support the library are through donations of time and money. Parents demonstrate how they care for their children's libraries by assisting in the maintenance of the collection and supplementing the acquisitions' budget. At the same time their personal values can conflict with school libraries materials' content. Their difference of opinion can lead to requests for withdrawal of materials they judge unacceptable. Such issues are presented in more details below.

LIBRARY SUPPORT

Parents are resourceful and they can strengthen relations with school boards and government officials to support schools and libraries by using strategies that can produce results. Some of them participate in budget meetings, write letters and call government officials to raise awareness about a school library's needs and difficulties. Also, they are directly involved in routine tasks or sporadic activities. Volunteering is their most visible form of contribution and it takes the following forms:

- Library Assistant
- Friends of the Library
- PTA & PTSA

Library volunteers are responsible for a variety of tasks determined by the librarian according to the most eminent needs. They provide assistance in programs and service areas, such as book fairs and shelving. They can contribute to a libraries' fundraising and collection maintenance efforts.

Friends of the School Library, the Parent-Teacher Association (PTA) and the Parent-Teacher-Student Association (PTSA) are organizations composed of parents, grandparents and even staff as volunteers. School libraries receive funds from these organizations to subsidize the collection, programs and even additional staff hours when needed. Their fundraising initiatives include membership drives, pasta feeds and auctions. The school librarian serves as a liaison providing input, presenting the needs of the library and requesting support.

Extra-Help Librarians interactions with volunteers are usually connected to the distribution of tasks and the supervision of work. However, it is of significant importance to know which of the organizations mentioned above are active in the school, acknowledge their contributions whenever suitable and also acknowledge individual volunteers' hard work.

Budget cuts accelerate the need for grants from other organizations to support extra activities that school districts are eliminating from a lack of funds. In such an environment, school libraries create grant proposals to supplement their acquisition budget and add programs that support the curriculum. Documentation is needed to demonstrate that the school library is essential to students' education. Extra-Help Librarians can assist in data collection to be used for budgeting and grant writing.

CENSORSHIP

Differences in values and a lack of openness to new ideas spark censorship initiatives. School libraries are often confronted with disputes about appropriateness and access to materials. For instance, with the expansion of the World Wide Web parents have raised the need for schools libraries to use filters in the computers to curb students' exposure to mature websites content, such as pornography and language. In case Extra-Help Librarians receive complaints about materials content or access to "inappropriate" websites, the knowledge of library guidelines on how to proceed is invaluable.

A library's collection access can vary among school districts, depending on a school's grade levels. Differences are more evident in schools with a wide range of grades, such as from kindergarten to the 8th grade, for example. Mixing young and older children in the same environment can raise concerns about the suitability of materials. Parents and guardians can be vigilant in protecting their children against what they consider unsuitable. Consequently, materials can be subject to grade level separation, become more difficult to reach or put in reserve. In middle and high schools due to the relative age maturity of students, items on sexuality or violence are likely to be considered not appropriate for their libraries.

Over the years some disputes have reached the Supreme Court and have become important cases. School libraries have been involved in many censorship challenges and some cases are listed below:

- Board of Education v. Pico, 457 U.S. 853 (1982)
- Bethel School District No. 403 v. Fraser, 478 U.S. 675 (1996)
- Campbell v. St. Tammant Parish School Board, 64 F. 3d184 (5th Circ. 1995)
- Case v. Unified School District No. 233, 908 F. Supp. 864 (D. Kan. 1995)
- Counts v. Cedarville School District No. 295 F. Supp. 2d 996 (W.D. Ark. 2003)
- Hazelwood School District v. Kuhlmeier, 484 U.S. 267 (1988)
- Virgil v. School Board of Columbia County, 862 F:2d 1517 (11th Cir.1989)

An Extra-Help Librarian's interest in staying abreast of censorship matters can benefit from The Scales on Censorship column of the School Library Journal. It focuses on current censorship disputes and provides answers to innumerable different situations. Also, learning about books that have been challenged, and promoting Banned Books Week by the ALA, can strengthen school libraries. Proactive ways to handle collection objections are to keep parents informed, listen to their concerns and follow necessary steps when disputes arise.

TEACHERS

Opportunities for librarians and teachers to work together are plentiful. However, professional cooperation requires time, planning, funding, staff and dedication. Note that community needs and administrative support are main considerations. A few examples of areas that these professionals engage in collaboration are mentioned ahead.

CO-TEACHING

The traditional roles of librarians in developing and maintaining collections and in teachers' positions are evolving. In school libraries the development of relationships with teachers is a major step in the process of classroom participation. Co-teaching in particular takes intensive coordination. It requires a comprehensive understanding of the responsibilities of each professional. Many factors influence the extent in which librarians and teachers collaborate. Elements that build a successful relationship include openness to experimentation and professional commitment. Other components that contribute to the development of a mutually beneficial partnership include the following:

- Vision and goals
- Leadership skills
- Knowledge sharing
- Clear communication
- Set responsibility areas
- Flexibility
- Program assessment
- Accountability
- Perseverance

Extra-Help Librarians working in schools with librarian-teacher collaboration programs are responsible for maintaining the equilibrium in place, careful not to strain the relationship. Boundaries are not always clear to those that are not directly involved. Consequently, it advisable to be even more sensitive to teachers comments in such an environment. In general, awareness of issues involving teachers and students may be key. For example, research by the Pew Research Center, accessible at http://www.pewinternet.org/~/media//Files/Reports/2012/PIP_TeacherSurveyReportWithMethodology110112.pdf, discusses the findings of research about elementary and high school students. Most importantly, it raises questions about who would provide the students with guidance in the process. It opens professional perspectives and motivates interactions with teachers.

Accepting long-term assignments in libraries where there is more demanding collaboration between the librarian and teachers, require much more involvement and focus to develop tasks. Consequently, clear knowledge of expectations and limitations of the Extra-Help Librarian's responsibilities can make it more manageable.

GAMES & CURRICULUM

Students' participation in the library requires a diversity of tools to motivate their curiosity in reading, math, history and other subjects relevant to their educational and social development. Traditional games such as trivia, challenges, puzzles and memory games have been available at school libraries, mostly for entertainment purposes. The introduction of computers in school libraries has generated new strategies to stimulate students' intellects. In particular, the integration of computer games into curricular activities is due to a strong belief in their educational value (Neiburger, 2007). Librarian-teacher initiatives on creating games are involving students in brainstorming, research, planning and design (Mayer, 2012).

Collaboration between librarian media specialists and teachers is important in modeling games that fit into lesson plans based on curriculum standards. New ideas adapted to students with different learning styles often use real world situations. The objectives are to increase digital literacy, problem solving skills, spatial skills, subject areas concepts and vocabulary. Other skills developed are how to follow instructions and leadership assertiveness. There is emphasis on confronting and overcoming challenges in a safe environment. Grade level and gender appropriateness, as well as content and goals are taken into account in the learning process. Gaming is a fun activity that provides opportunity for students to learn and at the same time builds skills and community.

Extra-Help Librarians in long term assignments might consider the school library's approach and use of games in curricular activities, such as Wii for math studies (Winner & Hearn, 2012). The professional's experience and/or open mind to plan and experiment are relevant in such a context.

REFERRALS

Librarians and teachers also have a role in coordinating referrals to other organizations. Relationships with public libraries, literacy leagues and tutors are ways to expand the net of support to their school community. Over the years connections between school and public libraries has been particularly strong. Directly or indirectly, school librarians and teachers refer students and parents to other resources at public libraries. Limited hours and materials are some of the determining factors.

The partnership of these libraries affects parents as well. For instance, when they seek tutoring information for their children and even themselves, they reach across libraries. Tutors maintain ties with libraries, using them as a source of referral and location to have tutoring sessions. Another resource is the Literacy Leagues which provide support to adults learning English.

On occasion an Extra-Help Librarian can identify patrons' needs not met at the school library and make referrals to other organizations. In addition, they are responsible for informing the absent librarian about it for further analyses and actions. Updating referral lists is a task that can also be a useful whenever there is a need or request for referrals.

STAFF

The importance of clear communication with a school's Principal and other administrative staff is a necessity at many levels. For instance, it is important to keep them informed about the library activities to encourage support. Counselors, nurses, speech therapists, administrative clerks and others are users and potential contributors, bringing new ideas and advocating for the library. The staff collaborates in the library's pursuit of value through their services and relationships. It is important that the Extra-Help Librarian understands staff's role in promoting the library. The services available to them serve as a link to strengthen the relationship and develop support.

Immersion Strategies

School librarians create close relationships with students actively participating in their growth as learners. For example, for years they guide them on their reading preferences. Naturally Extra-Help Librarians can face challenges to feel comfortable when temporarily replacing permanent librarians. Especially during short assignments, students are inquisitive and eager to know about what happened to "their" librarian. Excitement or discomfort can be generated by this new situation and new person, particularly by students in lower grades. Notification of changes in the library through brief class introductions and other forms of announcements often reduces the surprise factor and students can be more at ease. An Extra-Help Librarian's approachability is another facilitating factor. Conversations about class's interests and reading choices can lead to friendly connections. However, when confronting disrupting situations library rules should be enforced to curb students' misbehavior.

Also, open communication with administration at the school district and school site levels build confidence and improve outcomes. An Extra-Help Librarian's dialog with the principal, secretaries and teachers, as well as speech therapists and other professionals, contribute to camaraderie. Cooperation with the staff at meetings, as well as informal talks in the lunch room and hallways, can be of great advantage during transitions. A school's daily announcements and teachers bulletins are other helpful sources of information on current issues and upcoming events at the school.

The relationship between librarians, teachers and students has many implications on the library daily routine. Extra-Help Librarians' understanding of the interrelation of the tasks and the librarian in charge's management style and priorities, are necessary to reach the best results in the often limited time Extra-Help Librarians' may spend in temporary assignments at school libraries. Clearly, over long assignments there are more opportunities to introduce new ideas into the library activities, as well as develop connections with students, teachers, parents, volunteers and staff.

Extra-Help Librarians' knowledge of the work in general, and of specific tasks, improves their performance. Other skills—such as management of disruptive students, educational materials design, syllabus collaboration and presentations—can demonstrate abilities that are advantageous in school libraries. Their contributions can generate recognition of their worth.

CHAPTER REFERENCES

Byrne, Richard. (2012). Let's put our heads together: the best sites and tools for collaborative online studying. *School Library Journal,* 58, 4, Apr, 15.

Cummings, E. (2011). Assistive and adaptive technology resources. *Knowledge Quest,* 39, 3 Jan/Feb, 70-73.

Eberhart, G. (Ed.). (1991).*The whole library handbook: current data, professional advice, and curiosa about libraries and library services.* Chicago, IL: ALA.

Mayer, B. (2012). Get kids designing. Student created games combine curricular concepts and 21st century skills. *School Library Journal,* 58, 8, Aug, 22-23.

Neiburger, E. (2007). *Gamers… in the library?!: The why, what, and how of videogame tournaments for all ages.* Chicago, IL: ALA.

Neiburger, E. ((2007). *Gamers… in the library? Video games support the curriculum and develop a new form of literacy.* School Library Journal, 53, 7, Jul, 27-28.

Pew Research Center's Internet & American Life Project (2012). *How teens do research in the digital world.* Retrieved from http://www.pewinternet.org/~/media//Files/Reports/2012/PIP_TeacherSurveyReportWithMethodology110112.pdf

Williams, C. (2009, November 2nd). *Don't leave students without librarians.* Press Democrat. Retrieved from http://www.pressdemocrat.com/article/20091102/OPINION/911029937

Winner, M., & Hearn, M. (2012). Wii Learn. Surprise elementary grade students with a funway to learn math. *School Library Journal,* 58, 2, Feb.

Appendix A

SUBSTITUTE LIBRARIAN

The Adult Services seeks a dynamic self-starter to join its staff and serve the public at both its main and branch locations.

RESPONSIBILITIES/REQUIREMENTS
- State Librarian's Certificate
- County Department of Civil Service requirements must be met
- Provide all aspects of reference services using print and online resources (working knowledge of texting and familiarity with social networking sites required)
- Provide technical assistance re: use of public computers, scanners, downloadable collection
- Knowledge of MS Office
- Knowledge of Millennium (Innovative) a plus

HOURS

This is a substitute position.

Applicants must be able to work a flexible schedule including evenings, Saturdays and holiday weekends.

SALARY

$28.02 per hour

Recent MLS program graduates encouraged to apply.

Qualified candidates are invited to submit a resume and cover letter via mail, email or fax. This is an at-will position.

Appendix B

PART-TIME FACULTY POOL SUBSTITUTE LIBRARIAN

JOB NUMBER:

000

DESCRIPTION:

Serving as a substitute librarian, provide reference and public service to students, faculty and staff, utilizing print and electronic resources. Conduct library orientations and perform other related duties as assigned.

MINIMUM QUALIFICATIONS:

Education: Master's in Library Science, Library and Information Science OR The Equivalent.

Ability: Understanding of, sensitivity to, and respect for the diverse academic, socio-economic, ethnic, religious, and cultural backgrounds, disability, and sexual orientation of community college students, faculty and staff.

APPLICATION PROCEDURE:

To be considered for this pool, you must submit the following:

1. A completed application form
   (The only form of application accepted)
2. A current resume that details your education and complete work history
3. A cover letter
4. A separate document that provides information which demonstrates your understanding of, sensitivity to, and respect for the diverse academic, socio-economic, ethnic, religious, and cultural backgrounds, disability, and sexual orientation of community college students, faculty and staff.
5. Copies of all college transcripts
   Please note: If you are unable to attach your transcripts electronically, please have them available when interviewed.

Do not: Submit application, resume, cover letter or transcripts in paper form—they will not be accepted.

APPLICATION DEADLINE:

Community College District is establishing a pool of qualified applicants for Substitute Librarian. Applications will be accepted continuously until otherwise noted. Applications will remain on file for two years from the date it is received.

SELECTION PROCEDURE:

Applications will be screened by appropriate department representatives on an as-needed basis.

SELECTION PROCEDURE:

Applications will be screened by appropriate department representatives on an as-needed basis.

Qualified applicants who best meet the needs of the division will be contacted for an interview.

SALARY:

Education and accredited teaching experience determine placement on a non-negotiable part-time faculty salary schedule.

Appendix C

LONG TERM SUBSTITUTE – HS LIBRARIAN

JOB DETAILS

Job ID: Application Deadline: Posted: Starting Date:

Job Description Preference will be given to a state certified school librarian, who as completed a teacher preparation program educational degree, and holds a master's degree from a master's level program in school library and information studies.

Supervises: Paraprofessional(s) who comprise the school library staff, and, if applicable, volunteers, student assistants

Job Goals: To ensure that students and staff are effective users of ideas and information
To empower students to be critical thinkers, enthusiastic readers, skillful researchers, ethical users of information. To instill a love of learning in all students and ensure equitable access to information

JOB REQUIREMENTS

Teacher:
- collaborates with classroom teachers as a partner in the instructional process
- promotes a love of reading and lifelong learning
- promotes instructional technology to improve learning
- teaches students to build on prior knowledge to construct new knowledge

School Librarian:
- fosters a creative, flexible environment so that the school library is an essential part of the learning community
- develops and maintains resources appropriate to the curriculum, the learners, and instructional strategies of the school community
- evaluates, promotes and uses existing and emerging technologies to support teaching and learning
- promotes the ethical use of information: copyright, fair use, and licensing of intellectual property

Master degree preferred
Citizenship, residency or work VISA in United States required

Bibliography

ACRL Research Planning and Review Committee (2010). 2010 top ten trends in academic libraries: A review of the current literature. *College & Research Libraries News,* Jun, 71, 6, Jun, 286-292

ACRL Research Planning and Review Committee (2012). 2012 top ten trends in academic libraries: a review of the trends and issues affecting academic libraries in higher education. COLLEGE & RESEARCH LIBRARIES NEWS, 73, 6, Jun, 311-320

Automated scheduling saves Hennepin time. (2009 Jan/Feb). *American Libraries,* 40, 1-2, 87(1).

Bacon, P. & Bacon, T. (2009). *100+ literacy lifesavers: a survival guide for librarians and teachers K-12.* Westport, CT: Libraries Unlimited.

Belzer, S. (1936). The substitute librarian. *Wilson Bulletin for Librarians,* 11, Oct, 102-103

Berger, C. Strzynski, J. & Strable, E. (2002). *CBG guide for the interim librarian* (2nd ed.). Carol Stream, IL: Berger Group.

Bloom, L. (2008). NextGen: five tips to stand out. *Library Journal,* 9.

Branham, L. (2005). *The 7 hidden reasons employees leave: how to recognize the subtle signs and act before its too late.* New York, NY: American Management Association.

Brookhart. S. (2008). Grading (2nd ed.). Upper Saddle River, NJ: Pearson Education.

Caputo, J. (1984). *The assertive librarian.* Phoenix, AZ: Oryx Press.

Choltco-Devlin, B. (2007). Reference, passion, trust, technology. *Public Libraries,* 46, 3 May/Jun, 10-12.

Cohn, J. & Kelsey, A. (2005). *Staffing the modern library: a how-to-do-it manual.* New York, NY: Neal Schuman Publishers.

De Rosa, C. (2008). *From awareness to funding: A study of library support in America.* A report to the OCLC Membership. Dublin, OH: OCLC.

Disher, W. (2010). *Crash course in public library administration.* Santa Barbara, CA: Libraries Unlimited.

Evans, G. & Carter, T. (2009). *Introduction to library public services* (7th ed.). Westport, CT: Libraries Unlimited.

Farmer, L. (2012). Brace yourself. SLJ's school library spending survey show the hard times aren't over, and better advocacy is needed. *School Library Journal,* 58, 3, Mar, 38-43.

Ferrel, S. (2010). Who says there's a problem?: a new way to approach the issue of "problem patrons". *Reference & User Services Quarterly,* 50, 2, Winter,141-151.

Ford, C. (2008). *Crash course in reference.* Westport, CT: Libraries Unlimited.

Fourie, D. & Dowell, D. (2009). *Libraries in the information age: an introduction and career exploration* (2nd ed.). Santa Barbara, CA: Libraries Unlimited.

Griffins, J. & King, D. (2011). *A strong future for public library use and employment.* Chicago, IL: ALA.

Hall, M. (2003). Public to academic: reflections for librarians who are considering the switch. *Public Libraries,* 42, 3 May/Jun, 154-155.

Harvey II, C. (2011). An inside view of Lexile measures: an interview with Malbert Smith III. *Knowledge Quest,* 39, 4 Mar/Apr, 56-59.

Heintzelman, N., et. al. (2007). Cybertorials, teaching patrons anytime, anywhere. *Public Libraries,* 46, 2 Mar/Apr, 12-14.

Hogue, E. & Sisson, L. (1993). Part-time librarians: jewels of the profession. *Library Personnel News,* 7, 2 Mar/Apr, 7-8.

Hopper, L. (2010). *Boomers and beyond: reconsidering the role of libraries.* Chicago, IL: ALA.

Hughes-Hassell, S. & Harad, V. (2007). *School reform and the school library media specialist.* Westport, CT: Libraries Unlimited.

Institute for Career Research. (2009). *Career as a librarian, public libraries.* Careers No.8. Chicago, IL: Institute for Career Research.

Institute for Career Research. (2003). *Career as a school-college librarian: school media specialist.* Career No. 159. Chicago, IL: Institute for Career Research.

Intner, C. (2011). *Homework help from the library: in person and online.* Chicago, IL: ALA.

Jacobson, T. (2011). Facebook as a library tool: perceived vs. actual use. *College & Research Libraries,* 72, 1 Jan.

Johnson, D. (2003). Are libraries (and librarians) heading to extinction? *Teacher Librarian,* 31, 2 Dec.

Kenney, B. (2009). Happy days; despite the ups and downs, our satisfaction survey shows that librarians are crazy about their jobs. *School Library Journal,* 55.1, Jan, 28(4).

Khan, M. (2008). *The library safety and security guide to prevention, planning, and response.* Chicago, IL: ALA.

Knowledge Quest (2011). Educational Gaming. 40, 1 Sep/Oct.

Kranch, D. (1989). Automated scheduling systems: A comparison. *The Journal* (Technological Horizons In Education), 17.

    Kresh, D. (Ed.). (2007). The whole digital library handbook. Chicago, IL: ALA.

LaGuardia, C. & Oka, C. (2000). Becoming a library teacher. New York, NY: Neal Schuman Publishers.

Lindstrom, J. & Shonrock, D. (2006). Faculty-Librarian collaboration to achieve integration of information literacy. *Reference & User Services Quarterly,* 46, 1 Fall, 18-23.

Lowe, C. (2008). Rethinking the e-rate: the pros and cons of why libraries should be tapping the largest available pot of federal dollars. *American Libraries,* Oct, 62-64.

McCook, K. (2004). *Introduction to public librarianship.* New York, NY: Neal Schuman Publishers.

Milam, P. (2007). More than ever: why National Board Certification in Library Media is vital. In J. Repman & G. K. Dickinson (Eds.), School Library Management (6th ed.). Columbus, OH: Linworth Books.

Nicholson, S. (2009).Library gaming census report. *American Libraries,* 40(1/2), 44.

Primary Research Group.(2008). *Academic library website benchmarks.* New York, NY: Primary Research Group.

Primary Research Group.(2011-2012). *Library use of the mega-internet sites: Google, Facebook, Yahoo, Twitter, YouTube, Wikipedia, and more.* New York, NY: Primary Research Group.

Rivers, V. (2004). *The branch librarians handbook.* Jefferson, NC: MCFarland and Co.

Rubin, R. (2010). *Foundations of library and information science.* New York, NY: Neal-Schuman Publishers.

Scales, P. (2009). *Protecting intellectual freedom in your school library: scenarios from the front lines.* Chicago, IL: ALA.

Scales, P. (2009). When weeding is wrong: a principal asks for banned books to be removed from the collection. *School Library Journal,* 55.11, Nov, 18(1).

Shatkin, L. (2010). 50 best college majors for a secure future. Indianapolis, IN: JIST Works, Inc.

Shivani, V. (2011). Hitting the e-books. *Inc.* 500, 36, Sep.

Sommer, D. (2009). *Vault guide to library careers.* New York, NY: Vault.

Stim, R. (2007). *Getting permission: how to license & clear copyrighted materials online & off* (3rd ed.). Berkeley, CA: Nolo.

Sung, M. (2007). Ten tips for success: a new librarian's guide. *Public Libraries,* 46, 2 Mar/Apr, 42-46.

Winner, M. & Hearn, M. (2012). Wii learn. Surprise elementary grade students with a fun way to learn math. *School Library Journal,* 58, 2, Feb, 18-19.

Webliography

Academic and Research Libraries - ACRL. *A Guideline for the appointment, promotion and tenure of academic librarians.* Retrieved from http://www.ala.org/acrl/standards/promotiontenure

ACRL. *Awards programs.* Retrieved from http://www.ala.org/acrl/awards

ACRL. *Classroom control systems.* Retrieved from http://wikis.ala.org/acrl/index.php/Classroom_Control_Systems

ACRL. *Information Literacy Competency Standards for Higher Education.* Retrieved from http://www.ala.org/acrl/standards/informationliteracycompetency

American Library Association-ALA Accredited Schools of Library and Information Science Studies. Retrieved from http://www.ala.org/Template.cfm?Section=lisdirb&Template=/cfapps/lisdir/index.cfm

ALA. *Banned Books Week.* Retrieved from http://www.ala.org/advocacy/banned/bannedbooksweek

ALA. Code of Ethics. Retrieved from http://www.ala.org/advocacy/proethics/codeofethics/codeethics

ALA Connect. *Union.* Retrieved from http://connect.ala.org/node/71716

.ALA. *Libraries connect communities: public library dunding and technology access study 2010-2011 (PLFTAS).* Retrieved from http://www.ala.org/ala/professionalresources/libfactsheets/alalibraryfactsheet06.cfm#plftas

ALA *Code of Ethics.* Retrieved from http://www.ala.org/advocacy/proethics/codeofethics/codeethics

ALA Core *Competences of librarianship.* Retrieved from http://www.ala.org/educationcareers/sites/ala.org.educationcareers/files/content/careers/corecomp/corecompetences/finalcorecompstat09.pdf

ALA *samples of collection development policies.* Retrieved from (http://wikis.ala.org/professionaltips/index.php?title=Collection_Policies)

ALA *Social Networking: the state of America's libraries report.* Retrieved from http://www.ala.org/news/mediapresscenter/americaslibraries/socialnetworking

ALA *Unaccredited SLIS programs.* Retrieved from http://www.ala.org/offices/hrdr/educprofdev/nonalaaccredited

Arundel County. *Reemployment after retirement.* Retrieved from http://www.aacounty.org/Personnel/Pension/FAQReemployment.cfm

Badke, W. (2008).*Ten Reasons to Teach Information Literacy for Credit.* Online 32, 6 (Nov/Dec), 47-49. Retrieved from http://www.allbusiness.com/education-training/education-systems-institutions/11694245-1.html

Bellingham Public Schools. *Supervisor's resource bank: standards for teacher librarians.*

Retrieved from http://bellinghamschools.org/sites/default/files/departments/libmedtech/Supervisors/srblmsstandards.htm

Boroff, R. (n.d.). *Labor Unions - A Blessing or Burden?* Retrieved from http://ezinearticles.com/?Labor-Unions---A-Blessing-or-Burden?&id=6375766

Boyd, D. & Ellison, N.(2007). *Social network sites: definition, history, and scholarship.* Journal of Computer-Mediated Communication, 13(1), article 11. Retrieved from http://jcmc.indiana.edu/vol13/issue1/boyd.ellison.html

BridgeWater State University. *Faculty/Librarian Hiring Manual*. Academic Year 2011-2012. http://www.bridgew.edu/depts/acaffairs/Hiring%20Manual/Hiring%20Manual%202011-2012/Microsoft%20Word%20-%20Bridgewater%20State%20University%20Faculty_Librarian%20Hiring%20Manual%202011-2012.pdf

Burns, G. (1998). *Librarians in fiction: a critical bibliography*. Jefferson, NC: McFarland & Co. Retrieved from http://books.google.com/s?id=ryxP8KyrwswC&pg=PA127&lpg=PA127&dq=substitute+librarian&source=bl&ots=JjnZW4qbmw&sig=t7ZyBHEzv1UJFSkSxUyTX3zO2tc&hl=en&ei=_vFoS--KMYrCsQOWp-D1BA&sa=X&oi=book_lt&ct=result&resnum=4&ved=0CA8Q6AEwAzgo#v=onepage&q=substitute%20librarian&f=false

Campbell County Public Library System. *Collection development policy*. Retrieved from http://ccpls.org/coldev/

Common Core State Standards. *In the States*. Retrieved from http://www.corestandards.org/in-the-states

Consumer Reports (2012). *E-book reader buying guide*. Retrieved from http://www.consumerreports.org/cro/e-book-readers/buying-guide.htm

Cornell University. Library collection development. Retrieved from http://www.library.cornell.edu/colldev/cdhome1.html

Duncan, V. & Gerrard, A. (2011). All together now!: integrating virtual reference in the academic library. *RUSQ*, 4. Retrieved from http://www.rusq.org/2011/04/03/all-together-now-integrating-virtual-reference-in-the-academic-library/

Entertainment Software Rating Board (ESRB) http://www.esrb.org/ratings/ratings_guide.jsp#rating_symbols

Fargo Public Library. *Collection development policy*. Retrieved from http://www.cityoffargo.com/CityInfo/Departments/Library/AbouttheLibrary/PoliciesandProcedures/CollectionDevelopment-GeneralSelectionCriteriaandTools.aspx

Farkas, M. (Ed.). *Library circulating games*. Retrieved from http://www.libsuccess.org/index.php?title=Libraries_Circulating_Games

Hardenbrook, J. (2011). *Nailing the library interview*. Retrieved from http://mrlibrarydude.wordpress.com/nailing-the-library-interview/

Hartzell, G. (1997, Nov). The invisible school librarian: why other educators are blind to your value (Part 1). *School Library Journal*. Retrieved from http://www.schoollibraryjournal.com/article/CA152978.html

Hoover, S. (2009). Surviving your first library job search or, what I had to learn the hard way, reproduced here, for you, so that you are not driven to drink as well. *Library Journal*, Retrieved from http://www.libraryjournal.com/article/CA6697547.html?nid=2671&rid=#%23reg_visitor_id%23%23&source=title&

Internal Revenue Service. *Rules for retirees*. Retrieved from http://www.irs.gov/publications/p721/ar02.html#en_US_2011_publink1000228236

Iowa State University. *Advantages and disadvantages of eLearning*. Retrieved from http://www.dso.iastate.edu/asc/academic/elearner/advantage.html

Johnson, S. (2013). *Library job posting on the internet*. Retrieved from http://www.libraryjobpostings.org/all.htm

Kenyon College. *Collection development policy*. Retrieved from https://lbis.kenyon.edu/colldev/

Kumar, B. (2011). *What is the big deal with the "Big Deal"?* LibNotes. Retrieved from http://uccslib.org/libnotes/2011/08/24/whats-the-big-deal-with-the-big-deal/

Laura in Libraryland: a substitute librarian's survival guide. (Message posted on Dec 16, 2009). Retrieved from http://hr-hr.facebook.com/ALA.JobLIST/posts/207572603926

Librarian Substitutes 2.0 (2011). *Subbing in Hennepin County Libraries*. Retrieved from http://librariansubs.wetpaint.com/

Library of Congress Web Guides. *Library Listservs*. Retrieved from http://www.loc.gov/rr/program/bib/libsci/guides.html#listservs

Lorenzo, G. & Ittelson, J. (2005). An overview of e-portfolio. D. Oblinger (Ed.). *EDUCASE*, 2005. Retrieved from http://net.educause.edu/ir/library/pdf/ELI3001.pdf

Maatta, S. (2012, Oct). LJ's Placements & Salaries Survey 2012. *Library Journal*. Retrieved from http://features.libraryjournal.com/placements-and-salaries/2011-survey/the-long-wait-ljs-placements-salaries-survey-2011/

Maryland State Retirement Agency. *Reemployment after retirement*. Retrieved from http://www.sra.state.md.us/participants/downloads/forms/form_127.pdf

McNeil, B. & Gieseck, J. (2001). Core competencies for libraries and library staff. In *Staff Development: a practical guide* (3rd ed.). E. Avery, T. Dahlin, & D. Carver (Eds.). American Library Association. Retrieved from http://archive.ala.org/editions/samplers/sampler_pdfs/avery.pdf

Mid-Hudson Library System. *Public library policies & development tips*. Retrieved from http://midhudson.org/department/member_information/library_policies.htm

Mid-Hudson Library System. *Public library mission statements*. Retrieved from http://midhudson.org/department/member_information/missions.htm

Miller, R. (2011). LJ 2011 *Job satisfaction survey: rocked by recession, buoyed by service.* Retrieved from http://www.libraryjournal.com/lj/careerscareernews/890617-300/lj_2011_job_satisfaction_survey.html.csp

Morton Grove Public Library. *Collection development policy.* Retrieved from http://www.webrary.org/inside/colldevtoc.html

Occupational Outlook Online. *Librarians.* Retrieved from http://www.bls.gov/ooh/Education-Training-and-Library/Librarians.htm

Oliver, M. (2003, Jul 6). *Miriam Matthews, 97; Pioneering L.A. librarian was an expert in black history.* Retrieved from http://articles.latimes.com/2003/jul/06/local/me-matthews6

OPAL - Ohio Private Academic Libraries. *Weeding guidelines.* Retrieved from http://staff.opallibraries.org/resources/user_services/weedingguidelines.pdf

Osborne, A. (2007). *Library automation systems and vendors on the www.* Retrieved from http://members.iinet.net.au/~aosborne/vendors-systems.html

Phelps, S. (Ed.). (2003). Internet filters in schools and libraries. *Encyclopedia of Everyday Law.* Gale Cengage. eNotes.com. 2006. Retrieved from http://www.enotes.com/everyday-law-encyclopedia/internet-filters-schools-and-libraries

Primary Research Group (2010, May). *The survey of academic librarians: opinion of the usefulness of certain library technologies.* Primary Research Group, 75. Retrieved from http://www.researchandmarkets.com/research/f7f2ee/the_survey_of_acad

Stevens, J. & Streatfield, R. (2003). *Recruitment and retention.* SPEC Kit 276. Washington, DC: ARL. Retrieved from http://www.arl.org/bm~doc/spec276webbook.pdf

Turner, L. *20 technology skills that every educator should have.* Part 1. Retrieved from http://www.guide2digitallearning.com/tools_technologies/20_technology_skills_every_educator_should_have

Turner, L. *20 technology skills that every educator should have.* Part 2. Retrieved from http://www.guide2digitallearning.com/tools_technologies/20_technology_skills_every_educator_should_have_part_2

Turner, L. *20 technology skills that every educator should have.* Part 3. Retrieved from http://www.guide2digitallearning.com/tools_technologies/20_technology_skills_every_educator_should_have_part_3

The Economist (2011, May) *Academic Publishing*: of goats and headaches. Retrieved from http://www.economist.com/node/18744177

The University of North Carolina Greensboro. *The information literacy game.* Retrieved from http://library.uncg.edu/game/

Union - UFCW Local 1994. *Know your rights.* Retrieved from http://www.thelibraryunion.org/index.cfm?zone=/unionactive/view_page.cfm&page=Know20Your20Rights

University of Chicago. *Library mission, vison and values*. Retrieved from http://www.lib.uchicago.edu/e/about/mvv.html

University of Missouri. *K-12 library media specialist (LMS) certification*. Retrieved from http://lis.missouri.edu/certifications

University of Washington. *Policy for reemployment of librarians after retirement*. Retrieved from http://staffweb.lib.washington.edu/units/human-resources/current/retired-re-employeed/retire-reemploy-libn

Virtual Middle School Library. *Resources for school libraries – publishers and vendors*. Retrieved from http://www.sldirectory.com/libsf/resf/vendor.html

WebJunction (2009). *Competency index for the library field*. Retrieved from http://www.webjunction.org/resources/WebJunction/Documents/wj/Competency%20Index%20for%20Library%20Field.pdf

INDEX

A

Academic libraries, 107
American Library Association
    library schools accreditation, 1, 105
Archives, 100
Assigned projects, 49, 116
Association of College and Research Libraries
    academic library issues, 108
        association, 67
        awards, 83
        competencies, 118
        professional development, 31
Associations, 16, 66, 69, 83
Audio & video creation, 123
Awards, literary & professional, 82

B

Banned Books Week, 79, 84, 133
Benefits, 8, 30, 40, 43, 104
Book discussion, 57, 77, 81, 93, 97
Book fair, 81, 134
Booktalk, 142
Budget, 3, 15, 27, 29, 34, 42, 50, 54, 60, 69, 73, 87, 134, 144

C

Catalog, 53, 69, 94, 98, 102, 127, 145
Censorship, 2, 79, 146
Circulation, 52, 63, 73, 96, 137
Citation management, 121
Classification systems, 46, 135
Classroom management systems, 120
Collaboration, 55, 112, 117, 120, 123, 133, 137, 144, 147
Co-teaching, 133, 147
Collection
    development 3, 18, 50, 82, 95, 132, 142
    e- collection, 52, 54
    format, 52, 62, 95
    organization, 37, 46, 52, 94, 115, 135, 137
    selection, 51, 82, 88
    weeding, 55, 75, 137
Communication, 29, 33, 39, 47, 56, 60, 65, 68, 97, 116, 120, 142, 149
Computer filters, 103
Conferencing & presentation tools, 122

Content creation & sharing, 123
Content editing software, 123
Copyright, 57, 63, 80, 109, 116, 119, 122, 143, 154
Course/Learning management system, 120

D

Data collection, 50, 75, 146
Database, 54, 58, 75, 92, 96, 101, 107 113, 116, 120, 143
Dewey Decimal System, 46, 94, 132
Disability, 7, 76, 139
Diversity, 8, 76
Environment, 12, 27, 75, 90, 131
Statement, 23

E

Employment
    application documents, 22
    benefits, 8, 27, 30, 40, 43, 106
    considerations, 27
    prospects, 1, 40
    rejection notification, 24
    training, 4, 6, 9, 13, 30, 48, 54, 63, 78, 127
e-portfolio, 124
Equipment assistance, 57, 71, 75
Ethics, 36, 65, 122, 138
Events, 98, 133
Extra-Help Librarian
    profile, 8
    advantages, 11
    disadvantages, 15
    stress, 37
    responsibilities, 70, 131
    title terminology, 7, 106, 129
    union membership, 25, 43

F

Friends of the Library, Library Foundation, volunteers, 78, 87, 128, 132, 145

G

Gaming, 61, 77
Games & curriculum, 148

H

Homeschooling, 101
Homework help, 131

I

Immersion strategies, 149
Incident report, 48, 65
Information & learning commons, 117
Information literacy, 68, 105, 108, 110, 114, 118, 143
Interview planning, 21, 25
Institutional participation, 66
Intellectual freedom, 79, 88
Instruction, 3, 18, 25, 30, 41, 69, 102, 106, 108, 111, 114, 117, 119, 129
Instruction & technology, 119

J

Job Search
    application, 22
    categories, 6
    components, 19
    considerations, 18, 47
    description, 21
    documentation, 22
    interview, 26
    positions, 11, 89
    postings, 6, 14, 17
    pre-application, 18, 22
    references, 22
    strategies, 17, 20, 26
    structure, 89, 106, 128
    titles, 5, 7, 128
Journals & magazines, 67

L

Learning disabilities, 139
Librarian
    assigned projects, 49, 90
    benefits, academic, 106
    competencies, 4
    education, 1, 4, 8
    position titles, 5, 7, 128
    requirements, 20, 89,129
    responsibilities, 69, 110, 114, 129, 131
    services and priorities, 48
Library
    academic, 108
    catalog, 69
    hours, 38
    listservs, 68
    locations, 47, 89, 108
    mission, 46, 88
    organization, 88, 105, 128
    public, 3, 88
    school, 131
    services, 73, 94, 96, 108, 114
    support, 5, 78, 145
Library of Congress Classification, 46

M

Mathews, Marrian, 10
Marketing, 80
Master in Library and Information Science
    curriculum, core and elective classes, 2, 3
    students' learning opportunities, 4

N

New librarians, 9

O

Online classes, 2, 3
Online sources evaluation, 57
Organizational chart, 29
Outreach, 81

P

Parent-Teacher Association, 145
Parent-Teacher-Student Association, 145
Part-Time Librarians Association, 8
Patrons
    adults, 93
    assistance, 63
    children, 91
    faculty, 112
    local and global community, 113
    parents, 144
    potential problems, 63, 109
    seniors, 76
    staff, 113, 148
    students, 111, 13
    teachers, 147
    young adults, 92
Pay rate regulators, 29
Performance evaluation, 39
Plagiarism detectors, 122

Professional development, 29
Programming, 96
Promotional materials, 81
Public libraries, 87

Q

Quick response code, 125

R

Readers, 141
Readers advisory, 96
Reference, 115
Referrals, 148
Research, 142
Reservations, 72
Retirees, 9

S

Scheduling
    automated system, 33
    paper system, 31
    software, 34
School libraries, 127
Security & safety, 64
Seniors services, 76
Social networks, 59
Staff relations, 65
Student issues, 138
Survey creation & assessment, 124

T

Tax assistance, 100
Teacher certification, 129
Technical problems, 63
Technology assistance, 63, 71, 102
Time management, 35
Tracking statistics & feedback, 121
Transitioners, 10
Tutoring, 101

U

Union, 8, 29, 43, 78

V

Video hosting & sharing, 124
Virtual reference, 60
Volunteers, 78

W

Wages, 18, 27, 42, 107
Web 2.0 tools, 59
Websites, 57, 98
Work ethics, 36
Workers retention, 40

Acknowledgements

My sincere thanks to the people I work with at various libraries. A special recognition goes to the public, academic and school librarians who contributed to the improvement of this book. Also, I am grateful to my family for keeping us united especially during demanding times.

About the Author

Celma de Faria Luster has worked as an Extra-Help Librarian since 2007 and also as a part-time librarian since 2012. Her Master's in Library and Information Science is from San Jose State University. She also holds two undergraduate degrees from Brazil where she was born. She lives with her husband and their son in Northern California.

www.ingramcontent.com/pod-product-compliance
Lightning Source LLC
Chambersburg PA
CBHW080735230426
43665CB00020B/2742